LAPTOP THEOLOGIAN

LAPTOP THEOLOGIAN

SINCERE MINISTRY:
MINISTERING FROM THE HEART

REV. DR. LUONNE ABRAM ROUSE

LIBRARY OF CONGRESS CONTROL NUMBER: 2015913021

ISBN: HARDCOVER   978-1-5035-9470-8

SOFTCOVER   978-1-5035-9469-2

EBOOK   978-1-5035-9468-5

Scripture taken from the Holy Bible, New Living Translation, copyright 1996, 2004. Used by permission of Tyndale House Publishers, Inc., Wheaton, Illinois 60189. All rights reserved.

Scripture taken from the New King James Version. Copyright 1979, 1980, 1982 by Thomas Nelson, inc. Used by permission. All rights reserved.

Print information available on the last page.

Rev. date: 09/04/2015

To order additional copies of this book, contact:
Xlibris
1-888-795-4274
www.Xlibris.com
Orders@Xlibris.com
715852

CONTENTS

THE "GRACEFUL METHOD" IN SHARING FAITH IN GOD, JESUS CHRIST, THE HOLY SPIRIT, THE HOLY SCRIPTURES AND PERSONAL LIFE EXPERIENCES IS THE SINCERE PURPOSE OF A LAPTOP THEOLOGIAN. INVITING OTHERS TO DISCOVER A SACRED WAY TO SALVATION, WHICH IS LIVED DAILY IN PRAYER, BENEVOLENCE, SINCERITY OF HEART AND WALKING BY FAITH WITH HOPE OF UNDERSTANDING.

The purpose of this book is grief recovery. Human loss is unavoidable. It happens that we lose human beings to death and in living there are experiences of material losses that grieve hearts. Written through personal mourning of situational grief, the experiential stories are reflections on grief management and recovery with Biblical support. Throughout the entire work a psycho-social perspective on expressed grief is submerged into the valued and cherished key passages of the Bible.

It uniquely integrates the secular with the sacred for an ease into listening with compassion through various aspect of life as a means of grace to heal emotions and discover sustaining beliefs. Readers may read of versions of the Bible selected by personal choice. This author has chosen a variety of versions, including but not limiting the reader to the New Living Translation (NLT); New King James Version (NKJV) and New Revised Standard Version (NRSV).

There are many ways to help persons endure through death and dying. Why bring forth a refocusing method that brings belief in God, Jesus and the Holy Spirit into union with secular companions to make good of life's unavoidable difficulties as means of grief recovery? The answer is simple – refocusing works. Refocusing in a sincere ministry, because persons naturally help persons see what is human to see in the experience of living nights and days in grief recovery. Utilizing what is real and embedded within the human environment believers embrace faith, hope and love as objects present rather than attribute of the object desired.

A simple method in grief recovery care, because it can be a form of self-care. The methodology is a guide through situation loss and grief. It is unconditional and not situational specific. During good times or bad times, persons embrace the logic of the illogical and reduce emotional therefore think a new thing - refocus. Refocusing moves the human being to doing and moving onward. Logical that humans hurt from the loss and illogical that life is impossible without the object grieved, when life is still physically as well as spiritually possible.

Faith in search of understanding leads to refocusing on the attributes of God. Turning to God to overcome grief is illogical to the non-believer, but made to be logical to believer through faith, hope and love. Bible stories, therefore, gives valuable tools to help persons refocus from that which is beyond human control void of faith. Through the daily Scriptures and reflections persons reading this work shall in sixty-six days leave the former and step into the new.

An example of how it works may be seen in the following: If a person spends extraordinary time focusing on an alcoholic spouse or defiant child, it is instinctive to try to rescue until burnt out on failures. Human failures often drive persons into modes of depression, irrationality, anger, violence, and a variety of fear driven behaviors.

Committed reading and reflecting through this entire book may bring persons to refocus on things that are doable, manageable and affirming within a God focused and Christ centered life. The paradigm shift will change the process of recovery, for example: A Person focused on being hated responds out of defensiveness, having a blind spot to real problems, which may have or may not have anything to do with hatred. Refocusing on human responsibility and availability to caring for the wounds and hurts in the human experience shall prevent sickness of acting out, when breathing in and out love is the remedy.

Persons completing the reading of this book shall have opportunity to gain empathy. Readers shall gain an appreciation of the empathizing care offered by other persons, too. The book as accompanied by the Bible may turn negative lament into positive refocus.

Refocusing is sincere ministry: ministering with sincerity of heart grounded in the Biblical Word. The sixty-six books of the Bible read from a key chapter for sixty-six days is not a magical cure or mystical rescue. Rather, readers go to Bible passages for the purpose of satisfying the spiritual thirst for guidance in the search of understanding and finding a place of peace. Persons of all ethnicities are invited to refocus, for the book may be translated to appeal to people from all places in the world of every language, because the key guide is the Bible that has been translated into every language known to this writer.

This is the gem of refocusing in grief recovery within a sincere ministry: ministering from the heart – think through the moments, while sensing the feelings of those in your presence. Be not afraid to refocus the secular into the sacred, so as to meet the hunger and thirst of those grieving the loss they are meant to accept.

An example of refocusing the secular into the sacred, because all existence belongs to God: The fame singer and a former lead performer of the Beatles as well as Wings, Paul McCartney wrote and performed: "Let'Em In". Imagine joining in rendition of the hit song being sung at funeral or memorial services. Sensing the atmosphere, where people are open to the experience of transformation from despair with dignity toward rejoicing over lives well lived; such a song can become a voice calling to God. In some appropriate sittings, intentionally quote or sing portions of the song. Ending the funeral of one parishioner and slightly over two years later for his wife, who was even a more active member of our church, persons were invited into singing adaptations such as:

Someone's knocking at the door, somebody's ringing a bell.
Someone's knocking at the door, somebody's ringing a bell.
Do me a favor, open the door and let'em in. (repeat)

(adaptation inserting names of current deceased)
Uncle Jesse and Granny, too …

Someone's knocking at the door, somebody's ringing a bell.
Someone's knocking at the door, somebody's ringing a bell.
Do me a favor, open the door and let'em in…let'em in.

During the early movement of Christianity among Jews and Gentiles, believers required safe shelter, while representing Jesus Christ as the Way. Men and women challenged by cultural practices and spiritual understandings rose against followers of Jesus. The Book of Acts reports a scene where Paul, himself a Jew, was not able to bring a disagreeing crowd to peace. (Acts 19:21-41) Paul desired to push through the crowd to speak but was prevented by his supporters. Paul and Alexander could not represent the essence of the Christian movement over against the worship of idols. However, the city clerk brought human calm in the midst of the discord, when standing forward he became the respected source for the sake of human safety. In the end, he led the terrorizing crowd to a blessed dismissal and the assembly came to a halt. Through the coming years, Ephesus would become a place centered in Christianity not idol worship; even a place where the Virgin Mary is said to have lived and perhaps died. As children of God, stand firm on teachings of Jesus and in the end victoriously live. Brave are the men and women facing difficulty and threats of harm in the search for peace on earth.

Lula Alberta Woodbury Rouse, born on May 13, 1928, died on April 15, 2002. She was the first human influence on writing this book. She was my laptop theologian and taught biblical stories from her lap. Each story taught had a lesson of Jesus Christ, the Son of Man and Son of God. Often smiling, she would tell her three sons to "stick like glue, because Daddy and I will not be with you here on earth forever". On a Tuesday evening, she kissed this world goodbye. This book is in remembrance of the teachings from the sixty-six books of the Bible with emphasis on hope. The hope is that within sixty-six days readers may experience healing, sustaining, nurturing, and reconciling comfort during grief recovery. In the midst of pain and sorrow the essentials of faith and hope written in a "Sincere Ministry: Ministering from the Heart" has smoothing affirmation of love. One of Mother's favorite singers, Marvin Gaye, once delivered a song relevant for the ages: "What's Going On?" The reality of death and dying often becomes an existential request to know what is going on.

In the Book of Acts 19:21-41, people are brought to calm from outrage as the Kingdom of God was being established in Asia. Believers stood firm for righteousness and unity in the midst of diversity. People of God held to teaching on the assurance of eternal life. Even in the face of human death, believers held faith in being victorious and grew as spiritual champions. (Romans 8:37) The great experience of pain in losing beloved human lives is defeated by faith, hope and love. It is extremely painful losing lives deemed as essential to the human heart as breathing air. The essentiality of Christian faith is challenged by human death. The cessation of human life seems so final. How can it not be the end? What does it take for believers in God within the Christian community to inherit eternal life? What is eternal life? How does believing in eternal life help human beings, when beloved have died?

Jude, a servant of Jesus Christ and brother of James, urge believers in Jesus Christ to share "mercy, peace, and love" abundantly. (Jude 2; NKJV) Faith in Jesus Christ is a source of healing in times of dismay and sorrow. Eternal life is the gift of life extended to believers of Jesus Christ. (Jude 21) This teaching and understanding is embedded in this experience of God through these sixty-six days of readings. Eternal life is a heartwarming experience of living in the blessed assurance that Jesus Christ lived, died, arose and ascended. The promise is maintained in the spiritual power of the Holy Spirit - the essentiality of faith.

ACKNOWLEDGEMENTS

I acknowledge with joy the countless contributions to life that relatives, friends and advisors have granted. It was not predetermined that some would proceed into glory, while thoughts for this book were in the development phrase. Witnessing their progression through dying into death, I gained an understanding of feelings unknown to me. I thank God and those asleep until the coming of our Lord. Forty years of sincere ministry with people of God and we have new beginnings on the horizon; I am grateful to you among the living. I thank my wife for the expected encouragement and challenge to turn compassionate thoughts into expressed realities. Sharing in the essential times of need, it all belongs to God. With sincerity of heart I acknowledge that when I had decided to walk away from every aspect of the existence of this work, Marie said: "No, finish and glorify God by touching lives." Thank you, Holy Spirit, as you still every reader so as to know…

INTRODUCTION

From beginning to end, the Bible teaches that God the personal, living, creating God, is not simply the first principle of reality, the sustainer of the universe or a mere cosmic process but God is pervasive love, the rectifier of moral order, the evaluator of value. God, the ultimate in reasonableness, isn't merely a system of ideals. God is a responsive personal being who cares. God is the one who always relates and responds in love; therefore, God is the one who wills us ultimately only the good. (Major J. Jones)

THEOLOGICAL REFLECTION

"The thief's purpose is to steal and kill and destroy. My purpose is to give life in all its fullness." (John 10:10 NLT)

The body of Christ is to be strengthened, built, and made whole within an abundant life center (Howard Clinebell).

Have you ever considered establishing grief recovery ministries? Have you asked: How might a bereavement ministry begin and by what means in our local church?

In Pauline theology the Christian Church is described as the body of Christ (1 Corinthians 12:12-14). The identity as the body of Christ has do with the local church as a group of believers, who follow teachings of Jesus, so as to fulfill the mission of Christ in making disciples. Discipleship may include, but not be limited to celebrating the sacraments instituted by Jesus, such as baptism and the Eucharist; following the teaching and preaching of Jesus; and facilitating the mission and ministries of Jesus. The commission for discipleship is to build the Christian Church by making disciples, baptizing them in the name of God, Jesus and the Holy Spirit. Christians, then, are body builders, when they make disciples for Jesus Christ.

Christians may be body builders for Christ worshipping within and beyond the walls of local churches. However, a local church could be most effective, when body builders for Christ are providing abundant life ministries within and without the walls of the local church facility. Pastoral care is a ministry that could be rendered within and without walls of the local church. Pastoral care as a means of grace is effective in healing and equipping body builders for life. Body building as spiritually described may be compared to physical body building, in that the body builder may suffer wounds and experience grief.

PERSONAL REFLECTION

I practice as a Licensed Marriage and Family Therapist; Fellow in the American Association of Pastoral Counselors and United Methodist Pastor, who has faced the reality of being a "wounded healer." (Henri Nouwen) My brokenness in human relationships has resulted into periods of great grief. Yet during the same experience of life, my connectedness with God has solidified my human life as being unsurpassed in healing and reconciliation. It is by unbroken faith and love in God that my undeniable hope and daily assurance of blessedness and goodness are grounded. I am empowered through life experiences to lead therapeutic sessions in healing and supporting methodologies that foster mental health and spiritual development, too.

Ministry is service with an individual and corporate possibility. Christian ministry often has personal responsibilities, but never was intended to be void of laborers not just a laborer. Jesus Christ built a team of disciples and taught the soon to be Apostles the primary means of building the body of Christ – discipleship, a team approach to ministries. Wounded and grieved by the death and departure of Jesus Christ from human presence on earth, the disciples rose as a team.

The team approach to ministries led by wounded healers resulted into building the Christian Church. It is a model for leadership teams in local churches. Leadership teams are a means of grace providing hope for the development of abundant life centers in congregations and communities. Guidelines in responding to psychic, mental, spiritual, and emotional factors in human well-being are rooted in the theological ethos of abundant life centers. How are people guided into obtaining, sustaining and maintaining healthy human relations? Pastoral care and counseling may be the means of grace for human relations in experiencing the will of God in healing and training people of God. Persons may call the local church for pastoral counseling or training in care-giving. Fees may be accessed for both pastoral counseling and training ministries, especially when serviced by licensed professionals.

Desirable outcomes of an abundant life center (Clinebell):

1. To liberate, empower, and nurture wholeness centered in the Spirit;

2. To foster spiritual formation and ethical guidance in human lives;

3. To utilize and integrate both psychological and theological insights regarding the human situation, and the healing of persons;

4. To be holistic, seeking to enable healing and growth in all dimensions of human wholeness;

5. To nurture wholeness at each stage of the life journey;

6. To effect a reparative ministry of pastoral counseling;

7. To develop a shared ministry of care-giving with the pastor and the whole congregation;

8. To develop short term crisis intervention methods;

9. To become trans-cultural in ministries of the local church;

10. To enable people to increase the constructiveness of their behavior as well as their feelings, attitudes, and values is crucial in the helping process;

11. To utilize the unique professional identity and role of ministers;

12. To use intuitive, metaphoric, imaging approaches integrated with analytical, rational, intentional, and problem solving approaches in whole person transformation;

13. To become more effective in liberating wholeness in both men and women;

14. To provide growth-oriented psychotherapies;

15. To provide pastoral care in all the diverse functions of ministries, including preaching, worship, and social action;

16. To be effective growth-nurturer. (Therefore, the congregation is encouraged to support the continuing education of the entire staff)

THERAPEUTIC REFLECTION

Persons may participate in the above development by attending services, which are means of worship therapy, prayer therapy, music therapy, cognitive therapy, reality therapy, psychotherapy, medical therapy, marriage and family therapy, rational-emotive therapy, and much more.

"Who has anguish? Who has sorrow? Who is always fighting? Who is always complaining? Who has unnecessary bruises? Who has bloodshot eyes? It is the one who spends long hours in the taverns, trying out new drinks." (Proverbs 23:29-30 NLT)

Uncle Jesse was my ace. Alcoholism took him to an early death, in my opinion. Yet, the disease did not defeat our relationship. Our love for each other was greater than any smooth tasting wine and was always rekindled by the "new wine" Christ. In a real sense, he motivated my educational strives. He stopped by my room at South Carolina State College (University) during my first month as a freshman in 1973 to tell me: "Go straight through your four years and be the first male in our family to go straight through. Follow the example of your Aunt Ghussan not the males in our family and earn your doctoral degree. Do that for your Uncle Jesse." Then, he fell asleep on my bed, while I studied for my psychology class.

We faced challenges through the years. However, Uncle Jesse stayed with my family for a brief period of time through all of my educational experiences. Before he died I earned the degree as he desired. I never told him that my specialty as a marriage and family therapist is in the treatment of alcoholic families. Somehow that was not important information for him to know. What was important to him was that "we made it." He summoned me to visit him on his last days of life to say: "Thank you, we made it. I am going to die this time. Don't try to pray me back to life. But you know that I am proud of you. You go on and live for us. We made it."

Kathleen Sebelius, the Secretary of Health and Human Services, annually promotes the National Recovery Month. During September millions of individuals and families, "who have been through or currently are in treatment with recovery services for substance use and mental disorders," she notes, "celebrate recovery for themselves or a loved one."

The Substance Abuse and Mental Health Services Administration (SAMHSA) through its Center for Substance Abuse Treatment (CSAT) within the United States Department of Health and Human Services presents a toolkit to clergy and providers to help millions of our citizens with "facts and audience-specific information" concerning tools and educational material on substance use and mental disorders. If desirable, it recommended that you order kits at http://www.recoverymonth.gov/.

ADVOCACY REFLECTIONS

Leadership for sincere ministry is grounded in the Holy Spirit. Holy Spirit inspired leaders equips team members with armor for effective sincerity of heart ministries. Local churches should not diminish the active role of the Holy Spirit in the life of the congregation and community. The essentiality of the church is dismissed, when efforts to lead are void of faith in the supernatural influence. The differentiation between secular leadership and sacred leadership is the acknowledged power of the Holy Spirit.

The core challenge of leadership in the Christian context is to influence people to do effective sincere ministry for the church. When the local church is seen as another financial broker it loses the significance of being the spiritual fitness center, which Jesus arose to lead. Many local churches may be dwindling due to lack of influence in lead people to cooperate and take initiative on desirable outcomes working as a team.

When leadership relies primarily on socialization and modern technology for connectivity, frustration and disappointment are often the results. Leadership shielded with faith and glorifying God through intentional Christian service is most productive in fulfilling the mission of Jesus Christ.

Refocusing

1. How ready are team members for a sincere ministry in grief recovery?
2. To what extent are you equipped to create change?
3. Are some team members apparently more ready to lead than others? Why?
4. Based on your insight into what leaders have said, on a scale of 1 to 10 with 1 being unprepared and 10 being totally prepared rate the level of preparedness among your leadership to lead in the following:

    A. Ministry of Prayer
    B. Bible study
    C. Team Task Meetings

SINCERE MINISTRY: MINISTERING FROM THE HEART

Sincere ministry is sharing in the care of souls. Asserting self into situations needing your expertise is necessary to effectiveness. Sincere ministry is looked upon as a heart matter that is taken by a self-confident and assured individual.

Refocusing

Team members should discuss the following questions as a group.

1. To what extent has your heart blended into the church ministries?

2. Do team members appear to support one another on a fairly superficial level?

3. How can team members develop a more in-depth relationship personally and spiritually?

4. How can team member relationships be utilized in creating a sincere grief recovery ministry?

5. In what ways can team member relationships to God be used to maximize a sincere ministry?

SPIRITUAL FORMATION OF SINCERE MINISTRY

Much can be built on the sincere ministry inspired by the Holy Spirit. Spiritual Formation is a key to productive team management. First of all, team members should have a clear sense of the mission and its benefits.

Pastoral discernment is another key for team members in development and spiritual formation of sincerity of heart ministries.

The spiritual formation requires personal responsibility as well as personal accountability.

Self-denial is too often overlooked in the development of spiritual formation among team building, so be intentional in sincerity of heart ministries. Collective and individual practice of self-denial is important in building a sincere ministry.

REFOCUSING

1. The kingdom of heaven belongs to those who are seeking to be blessed spiritually and economically. The church should be a spiritual fitness center and economic development institution. Spiritual champions live to strengthen the weak in spirit with manna from the Spirit and human resources. In this kingdom, God reigns supreme over all the earth. Spiritual champions understand that for the minds to digest the spiritual, the stomach needs to digest solid food or the sounds of noise from the stomach may even drown out the sounds of music in worship.

2. Spiritual champions are sinners saved by grace. They mentor persons, who are mournful and crying in brokenness.

3. Spiritual champions understand that there is more to life than personal holiness, because there are tears over social ills as well.

4. Spiritual champions seek not to bring drama. Rather, as champions rejoice in loving others by not getting high on self-love. Humility is a virtue all must strive for and uphold in living the righteous life.

5. Hungering and thirsting to do the things right in life, spiritual champions live to obtain mercy with purity of heart participating in the makings of peace throughout the world.

6. Living the righteous life is the goal of Spiritual Champions against all adversity, including those who would persecute or seek the destruction of the Church as the body of Christ.

Prayer: Lord Jesus Christ, Son of God, have mercy of my sinful soul. Amen.

All within being human is due to the Being of Existence. The question of being in the world is an ontological essential. Rene Descartes, (1596 - 1650), placed rational knowledge at the root of existentialism as opposes to information received through senses. His famed philosophical gem is cogito ergo sum, meaning "I think, therefore I am." Descartes in the mindset of most scholars went too far in downplaying the physical world, still his stress on subjectivity and individuality has influence the philosophy and theology of existential being. While Descartes has forever been rooted within, it is the work of Soren Kierkegaard (1813-1855), Paul Tillich (1886-1965), and increasingly Edmund Husserl (1859-1938) that impacts writings of the laptop theologian. The challenge contrast between rational knowledge and "sense data" motives a deeper search for peace.

The Husserl concept of intentionality is as a state of consciousness in awareness of something, which consciousness is always in a state of awareness. Within current thought is the search for peace through faith in the intention of divine creation. God had an intentional beginning and has an eternity intention that will not be denied believers though interrupted by the sin - estrangement that creates angst. Existence allows human beings to exist in reality. Blessed human existence is confirmed by conscious awareness of existing in affirmation of the intentionality of the Creator of life, which is Existence that I have learned to call God. In reality, grace is the characteristics of God known by mere human existence.

In response to a sermon her parents heard preached at a funeral of a friend, a girl was brought to baptism. When the eulogy was delivered, I barely knew our mutual friend. However, the means of grace in our mutual existence affirmed a birth as much as it confirmed an existence beyond death. In all that we say as well as in what we do may there be divine intervention, so that grace and mercy bring us to an appreciation of existence. By the grace of Existence, dare to believe you exist because Existence is in you, so as to know without doubt you exist in Existence.

13

SELF REFLECTIONS

In 1995, Ray Sherman Anderson wrote a book on Self Care: a theology of personal empowerment and spiritual healing. The focus on self is important for pastoral care and counseling. Knowing about the self and how God empowers human beings into a divine image are keys to effective shepherding. Self-care has to do with experiencing self-worth, building emotional health, and embracing a vital faith. Henri Nouwen became known for his many works on solitude. One of them geared especially toward priest is his work on The Wounded Healer. Both of these gentlemen point out from a protestant and catholic perspective, respectively, the reality of human hurt that is experienced in the lives of servants and shepherds. The works give insight into how healers serve through the pain of personal wounds.

Out of the experience of lost, hurt, and abuse may come a shepherd to attend to the flock appointed by God. It is done not in arrogance or sense of superiority. Rather in the discovery of authentic self-experiences of wounds and the healing of wounds, pastors accept the empowerment of God to work beyond brokenness. Clergy and laity may come to know the reality of healing, guiding, sustaining, reconciling and nurturing as defined by Howard Clinebell in the Basic Types of Pastoral Care and Counseling.

HISTORICAL REFLECTIONS

September 11th carries deep pain for so many people in the United States of America, especially in New York. Time has passed, since we gathered in Heckscher Park of Huntington, New York to remember the lives lost years ago. The disheartened attacks in New York City in September of 2001 changed human interactions throughout the world. On that day known as 9/11, eyes were filled with tears, voices resounded from cries and prayers uttered remembrance...

"For God so loved the world that he gave his only begotten Son, that whoever believes in Him should not perish but have everlasting life. Indeed, God did not send the Son into the world to condemn the world, but in order that the world might be saved through him." (John 3:16-17 NKJV)

Two days into 2012 and the voice on the twelfth phone call of the day spoke love as real as ever. Unexpected a few years ago, yet as promised over three decades ago love doesn't change though people do. Divorced after decades of marriage and having to hear people of the world say: "Get over the dog that has done you wrong." "Go on with your life." "You deserve better." Such words, even with good intentions are not pastoral. Pastoral words are given with respect and care for the thoughts and emotions of the hurting not for the ones intending to console. When caring for the broken in heart, listen with empathy.

COUNSELOR REFLECTION

Hearing the voice on the other end of the phone is not always easy when you are in the deep rivers of responsibilities brought in with the New Year. Pastoral counselors, for sure, have to take care to be able to care for the souls of men and women. When pressures on the emotions of the counselor are too severe, the counselor needs to make clear the unavailability to attend to the needs of the persons in stress. Not intending to blow the opportunity to help, pastoral counselors should prayerfully pause and make sure to be available in authentic ways to the person or persons needing them. The caller had questions. While the caller did not need to hear the response of a pastoral counselor, the needy needed the pastoral counselor to be able to respond with true answers.

Things happen to good people in life, which are not so good. Searching for answers to why things happen is the nature of being human. Pastoral words to the hurting are meant to heal, guide, sustain, and in some cases reconcile. Words of truth should be pastoral, and you do not have to speak as a pastoral counselor to speak the truth in love. How do you tell love of years past that God has to make something out of the non-sense? While it is human to search for answers, it is human, too, not to have the answers desirable in the search. When you have searched and searched, cried and prayed; searched until you cried and cried through your prayers, you hold on to faith, hope and love.

God does love the world and gave Jesus Christ, so that by believing we shall receive. The answer is in life, and the life of believers is eternal. What may not be clear today shall be made clear by and by. Wait on the Lord, who gives all things to those who trust and obey.

Well, the answer has been found. Pray in the name of Jesus Christ, our resurrected Lord through all human hurt. When we pray the answer may not come from the source of inquiry but from God, and be given to both the researcher and the interviewed. Beyond every intentional question of why, there is an intended response for relief. God has the answer as revealed through Jesus Christ. "For this, too, he died." Forgiveness comes when the answers given in truth are the pastoral words representing God. God is gracious and merciful, righteous and good, so that even the disrespectable actions are forgiven as the reverence to God is given. The answer is wrong and cannot be made right, but shall be forgiven, so that the children of God may process and step in the blessedness of reconciliation with God through Christ. The human to human relationship in the end fades by numerous means, but the Divine to human relation as with love cannot be changed though people do.

Prayer: God of grace and righteousness, have mercy on us and grant us goodness with forgiveness, so as to be at peace within. Amen.

1. We must enter into a discernment process and carefully examine our future in bereavement ministries as a church, if we do not change. Develop a list of 10-20 critical measurable points which our effectiveness as a church within may be defined? Utilize this information to see why the local church could be more successful than other sources in grief recovery.

2. We need to be open-minded and receptive to new ideas. The outcome of the bereavement process may lead into new ways of ministry and serving the people of God to grow disciples of Jesus Christ.

3. We acknowledge that all members of the church, regardless of where they may be in their stage of life, must have a voice in our new direction as we build our bereavement ministries. What are some of your suggestions for grief recovery ministries?

GRIEF RECOVERY MINISTRIES has the purpose of refocusing Christians on living in accordance with the will of God through circumstances and conditions of living. Christian behavior is crucial to positive grief recovery.

Day 1

WHAT DO YOU THINK?

Read: Genesis 12-15

Grief by any definition denotes love in sorrow. Sadness and extreme pain is felt with sincerity of heart. The source of grief is the object of desire. The cause of grief is the perception of the source. The feeling of grief is the awareness of love. The consequence of grief is the response of sincerity. Grief responders search for the source believed to be loved with sincerity of heart. What do you think?

"When my wife hurts, my heart hurts, too"; he said. "Perhaps every man feels this way. I don't know." (Pause) "I never meant for her to hurt. Never would I intentionally hurt her or allow someone to cause her pain. She has to know that my love is real. When things go wrong, it is a reality that the heartbreak is mine. I mean, deep, deep inside my heart is broken every time her heart is hurt, especially when the cause of hurt has to do with me. (Pause) "What do you think?" A mentor in the latter years of ministry said, "The only failure we have is not to try." It is a caregiver's responsibility to try with sincerity of heart to care for souls.

Try comforting a person, when their spouse is at a distance and they sense love, if not lost, to be hurting and you may discover the role of pastors and pastoral counselor and lay caregivers in the Christian context. What do you think to say or have a person in grief do, when they are sensing lost? Clergy or lay caregivers in sincere ministry accept the opportunity to be responsible in the moment. Deep in the heart is a desire for all people to recover from grief without overvaluing thoughts or devaluing feelings. "What do you think?" is the question posed by a hurting spouse. In sincere ministry, caregivers may listen to hear the grief and speak from a position of caring not authority. Recently, reading a book about lay care-giving training for various ministries of the church encouragement came to this avid reader to engage in the process, while leaving the results to God.

Engaging the hurting spouse with deep compassion and sensing the pain of agony in the case above an effective response could be: "Speak of your hurts and fears of rejection. You have a responsibility to be available to your wife, so as to say what you are thinking and feeling within, so what are you thinking? What hurts are from lack of courage to seek forgiveness? What hurts are surrendering to the fear of being rejected? Speak of wisdom urging you to offer unconditional love in hope of receiving love unconditionally. Grief hurts and heartaches challenge the entire human system at times. A lack of heart to be compassionate is yielding an experience of pain. A love feast is desired in hopes of forgiveness and reconciliation. When are you going to your wife? What do you think? Dry your tears and say: 'I am done with thinking. I am going to find my spouse. I will ask the one person I love as the very life of me: 'Darling, will you please come home? You are the key to my happiness.'"

PRAYER: "Lord Jesus Christ, Son of God, grant mercy and healing upon us, who grieve. Amen."

Day 2

ADVERSITY HAS AN END

Read: Exodus 12-14

"God will not place on you more than you can bear." What a phrase. The interpretation may vary from person to person, but the essence of the statement remains the same - adversity has an end.

A few years ago, while going through painful days in prayer retreat seeking God's will, a valley experience overwhelmed the soul. Interestingly, there was a place of peace accessible by public transportation. Safe walks through the parks, bus rides, train hops and air flights. Whatever it took to survive was tried. Going through difficulties and working it all out was very challenging. The challenge was made least cumbersome by the ways and means of refocusing. Retreating from stuff and refocusing gave respite and strength needed to move onward.

Refocusing held fast to days of going back to basics with limited cell phone use and computer access. Prayer was a key in refocusing through long days and some sleepless nights. Stepping away from the burdensome tasks was the best part of the divine treatment plan. Internal debates welcomed and unwelcomed pursued. Glances into the past were unavoidable, yet built confidence in visions of the future. The message that resonated at the core of being was: "Days of excellence shall come and the adversity shall cease." Until then, continuous songs of praise shall anchor the soul in our Lord.

What are you taking for the pain in your life? Is your faith-grounded, during the storms of life?

Refocus on our Lord by accepting eternal life through faith in Jesus Christ. Live into the Christian basics of spiritual disciplines. The adversary remains active during such time and evil appears to be winning, but the victory is guaranteed in Jesus. The ending of the story is in the glorification of God. Trust in the restoration power of our Lord, who overcame death on the third day morning through the same power of God that restored life to a suffering Job. God is more than able. The Almighty is a true Promise Keeper. When all has failed and the enemy encamps against us, turn around and seek the face of God. God is with us; the adversity has an end.

During refocusing prayers, strength was gained through repeating the words of 2 Chronicles 7:14: "If my people, who are called by my name will humble themselves and pray and seek my face, and turn from their wicked ways, I will hear from heaven, forgive their sins, and heal their land." The recipe during times of adversity has within it repentance and daily prayer to the God of restoration. Following the recipe, refocus and believe excellent days shall come.

PRAYER: "Lord Jesus Christ, Son of God, grant mercy and healing upon us, who grieve. Amen."

Day 3

A Love Centered Life

Read: Leviticus 16-17

A woman cried today. It was not the first time she has cried. It may not be the last time she cries. It is one of the times she cries for her loved one, who died one week before the floodgate of tears exploded in her life. Reality of love and certainty of lost were expressed through tears while planning a service of remembrance.

In the midst of tears she spoke: "my precious beloved", she said, "was a nice man, husband and father. You would have enjoyed meeting him." He was introduced that day through a loving wife. From her spoken words, the eulogy was designed around the anatomy of the idea: "A man and husband, who lived the character of a child of God." A middle aged woman, living a love centered life with her husband was facing the question: "How do I live without him?"

She enjoyed the unconditional love, which her intimate friend delivered. He gave daily positive regard from his whole heart. His illness brought challenging times. Still, in sickness he dedicated himself to working for the benefit of his wife and their children. Once he could no longer move from the bed and impending death kept him from working, love remained solid as a rock. Their marriage and family gave testimony to a love centered life grounded in mutual respect and self-sacrifice.

Imagine merging a love centered life with a Christ centered life. Think about it. Pray for it. It could be the joy of loving God with total self-control and loving your spouse with total self-discipline. Spousal love is godly, when lived in respect to the principles taught by Jesus. Christian loving is expressive through service. It is a service of sacrifice and inconvenience, which is centered in mutual exchange; loving the other as loving oneself. A Christ centered life is love in keeping the commandments of Jesus (John 14:15).

Getting right down to it, the essence of love is in the daily remembrance and appreciation of who you love. Every day is a loving day; a time to remember the precious love granted by God to be shared in the spiritual and physical. Loving God is not exclusive of loving humans; it is in loving humans within the principles of God that we experience the mutuality of godly love, which is a character that never dies.

A woman cried today; God dried her weeping eyes.

PRAYER: "Lord Jesus Christ, Son of God, grant mercy and healing upon us, who grieve. Amen."

Day 4

BELIEVE IN THE PROMISE

READ: NUMBERS 14

Local church mission statements express hope in fulfilling the biblical image of the Church as a "body of Christ." Members of local churches make individual confessions and collective commitments to live in unity striving to fulfill the mission.

Adopting a Pauline theology, members in a local congregation pooled individual gifts into a practical treasury to fund extension of ministries beyond facility walls and into the building of the body of Christ into the community. Christian church facilities are often centers of worship, where praise and prayers are lifted for spiritual growth. Development of ministries in local churches has the purpose of meeting human concerns. Focusing on God as Creator and Redeemer, worshippers gather for praise in thanksgiving with supplication and continued compassion. Compassionate care, love, empathy and respect of humanity are gifts from God expressed through effective ministries of local churches.

The essential task in local church is representing divine unconditional love. Divine love is expressed through acts of compassion. Members are taught that the desirable outcome of all actions has to do with the well-being of people of God. Therefore, on every age-level and through all areas of the local church the following acts are life sustaining:

1. Acts of kindness. In the tradition of the Methodist Movement (many faith communities share this basic view), persons are taught to "do no harm." This is the first step of three in principles of Christian living taught from the heritage of John Wesley, often regarded the father of Methodism. Persons of faith place their unwavering trust in the grace of God. Non-violence is discipline of ideal living. Acts of kindness includes

non-violent following of Jesus Christ. Trusting God as the giver of life, Christians strive to fulfill the mission of Jesus Christ in the world. It is the faithful privilege of the disciples of Jesus. Avoiding harm and evil of any kind, Christians request removal of violence a resolution to conflict. Believing the cost of discipleship has been paid fully by the sacrificial love of Jesus, Christian disciples walk fearlessly liberated in the world. Though challenged by the evil that exists in the world, believers live by faith (radical to the ways of world) seeking ways and means of peace. Christians render acts of kindness toward believers and non-believers. The lives of Christians speak of Jesus Christ.

2. Acts of generosity. The intentional means of doing good deeds for others. A universal application of gentleness and respect of anyone and anything challenges a child of God to practice positive regard. Worldwide love, even of enemies, is in the mission of Christian disciples. Acts of generosity and hospitality are expectations of faithful discipleship. Pathway of Jesus Christ is paved with generosity and servant hood. True rendering of Christian service is not prejudicial. Generosity is expressive of the personal relation with Jesus Christ in service within and beyond walls of the church building. It is the act of giving, because one has been given the love of God.

3. Acts of love. The mind, heart and soul abide in the teachings of Jesus. Life at its best is lived respecting, listening, caring, and empathizing with people of God. Loving God and neighbor. Visible care expressed in words and actions. It is impossible to love God and not love the creation of God. Loving God is faith in action with hope in peaceful existence with others. Loving God is attending to the ordinances of God.

When the three rules are made plain, then the Body of Christ continues transformation in the world through the power of the Holy Spirit. Building the of body Christ by sharing the faith, Christians are "BODY BUILDERS OF JESUS CHRIST".

PRAYER: "Lord Jesus Christ, Son of God, grant mercy and healing upon us, who grieve. Amen." 🖊

Day 5

COVENANT RENEWAL

Read: Deuteronomy 27

Moving from South Carolina to New York was a response to a divine call. The purpose was to revitalize an inner-city congregation. The sacrifice was distance from family and friends. Daily routines, rituals and issues were different. However, the diversity between metropolitan East Harlem, NY and Marion, SC are not intended for tragedy, per se, in Christian ministry. Sincere ministry in every Christian context has adjustments in accord with age level differences. As the frequencies of persons dying, being available and responsible for officiating funeral services drastically increased.

Having studied gerontology as well as seminary training was helpful, no doubt. Yet, no preparation for pastoral care was more important than love for people. Persons are dying at the moment human life begins. Before the first breathe until the last breathe leaves the body, people by any name can benefit from pastoral care, which is inclusive of the full range of emotional and spiritual grief. Sincere ministry in the south or north as in the east or west is an explainable reality acceptable in the face of death and dying. Death and dying is a human commonality in the midst of diversity. People live and they die regardless of the differences in human experiences. Life that is breathed in will one day breathe out and return to the eternal source. Ecclesiastes 12:7 acknowledges that dust (the body) returns to the ground, and the soul (breath) returns to the God, who gave it. How effective is pastoral care during funerals, memorials and resurrection services?

Death is not a friend to life. In fact, death removes friends in life. When someone dies it is a reminder that the human experience is one of cessation. Pastors, too, are human beings living in the midst of dying and may have moments of hurt, during the death and dying of parishioners. The mind, heart and soul may appear as waterfalls as the impact of death brings feelings to mind and sense of lost to the heart. When death is experienced a sincerity of heartfelt ministry does not have to be denied. While Christian theology provides an image of eternal life and peace, the message does erase loss of human life. What are effective pastoral responses to death and dying?

In waiting, may there be the assurance of eternal life. With Christians awaiting the Parousia (Second Coming of Christ), there is a reality of love and struggle with human lost. Being able to communicate pain in safe environments, feeling the compassionate touch of friends and the ability to cry out emotional pain may in time help the healing process. Death comes to all, but belief and trust in God guarantees the life beyond death. When death comes, our lives continue with God, who is Alpha and Omega.

PRAYER: "Lord Jesus Christ, Son of God, grant mercy and healing upon us, who grieve. Amen."

Day 6

Win the Prize

READ: JOSHUA 24

We will all face death. The cessation of life is assured. Unless the Savior comes and raptures the people of God with a last breath human beings will die. Still, there is a promised life beyond death. Let us press on to win the prize of eternity.

The news media announces deaths, which are of public interest. Political leaders, celebrities and deaths of any person involving criminal intent are often quickly reported.

On the morning of August 26th, an announcement of death came by news media. Cancer has to do with an infectious illness that is fatal, if not conquered by human medicine. Through a natural process of treatment or conventional acts of medical doctors people are provided care until death. In my mind, I thought of cancer survivors and those dying by cancer. I thought of health care, civil rights, education, and fair treatment of people and of the ending of life.

I surmised a person of interest and intelligence; wounded and deeply sorrowed more than once is life fulfilled the call of service in humanity then died. While human loss saddens, weep not the death of another without preparing for your own. In facing death, imagine the soul rising from the bed in reach for a place of eternity.

People may speak immeasurable contributions in the aftermath of deaths. All tributes deserved and well made. Remarks of historic living may be made by admirers. However, history cannot record the final story.

The final story is beyond human history. History reports what has been "history". What history cannot capture are the records of eternity. Human beings can only speak in hope of knowing an eternity free of discord and filled with peace. In the end, the same hope for human souls is lifted for the dead in Christ to win the prize!

PRAYER: "Lord Jesus Christ, Son of God, grant mercy and healing upon us, who grieve. Amen."

Day 7

SOLITUDE WITHIN A 5-POINT CYCLE

Read: Judges 2

Jesus went away from the crowd in solitude. What is solitude? What happens in solitude?

Solitude is a place of awareness. The place where the mind photographically and experiential captures the reality of being now. Solitude is the place where yearning thoughts feast on the imaginable perfection hoped for, yet to be realized. In a real sense, solitude is the place of dreaming the impossible into possibility, so as to become motivated to reach for the unreachable. It is solitude in that a person of faith may come to the conclusion that there is unending array of possibilities, which cannot be accomplished by inactivity but requires action. For Jesus, according to John 6:15, there was a time of departure unto a mountain to be away from the crowd. He drifted away from the doing of things. Having met the physiological needs of people, Jesus sought to be in solitude, alone to be restored in power and holiness. I believe he was in a HOLY PLACE being in solitude, because holiness was in him refueling Jesus with divine power to face the needs of humanity. Holiness and divine power are needed in the world. Where do you go, when you need power and desire holiness?

The Word in John 6 reminds us that we are to follow Jesus for the right reasons, the reasons being spiritual and physiological. While the Lord provides strength, which we use to meet needs of shelter, food and clothing, we are taught that as the eye of God is on the sparrow and the Lord watches over humanity in every manner of need, including the soul. Jesus lifts up unto us a greater purpose for being in His entourage, which is feasting on the spiritual manna of the Word. He institutes a call to the holy feast. The institution of the Eucharist in John 6 brings to our full awareness the responsibility of abiding in Christ and having Christ abide in us.

The Holy Table; Holy Communion Rail; The Altar by any name may be a place of solitude. Partaking of the Holy Eucharist around the holy table is a place of communion, a place where God may be encountered or experienced in a way that leads to forgiveness and reconciliation has power and by the means of grace a resource of holiness. A spiritual awe comes through bread of reconciliation and wine of peace. It is in solitude that the feeder is fed, in order to gain strength to feed humanity. You are not required to be the preparer or the primary source of giving in solitude. In solitude you are cared for so as the recipient of authority come out of solitude and adorned in holiness to care for the people of God.

However, solitude as personal as it is with God can never be a rationale for solitary Christianity. No, no, no it is not a personal religion without need for fellowship or discipleship. It is not a lone ranger trip or non-church journey into spirituality. Solitude is the place of fueling within the Body of Christ, not away from Christ in the world today. It is the spiritual station that is as important to soul as the gasoline station is to an automobile. In solitude you are filled up not to stay at the station or hold on to the fuel. You are to come out of solitude filled and rekindled so as to keep the charge of love. In solitude, I discovered the 5-point cycle of life moving around sin, servitude, supplication, salvation and silence.

PRAYER: "Lord Jesus Christ, Son of God, grant mercy and healing upon us, who grieve. Amen."

Day 8

BREAD OF LIFE

Read: Ruth 4

Do you feel the need for rekindling? Ruth felt the need to rekindle following the death of her husband born of Naomi and was found to be a root of the very essential existence for the world. Jesus!!!

Do not go on vacation from God; God never vacations from you.

Come into solitude and be nurtured by God, so as to spread the love of God unto others. When the need for power and holiness is felt, journey into solitude to refuel for the purpose of being effective in Christian service. Then, go beyond the walls and into the mountainous areas of human need and care for mind, body and soul of people of God.

What happens in solitude will be personal experience. Faith-sharing is witnessing to the personal encounter, so as to testify to the great change available for all responsible beings. It inspires love of every person through sincerity of heart. These are not mere words speaking of ways and means ordinary people are not capable of obtaining. These words witness to the ability of strangely warmed hearts caring for strangers in the human experience of life. People come from every walk of life. They crowd into the city. They are all around at all times. The challenge is to find through solitude the strength for the multitude of persons in need. Faced with opposition, Jesus stakes his claim for faith. Picture the faces of those following Jesus to Capernaum, when Jesus called them out as following for wrong reasons. Jesus tells them to work for the bread that endures forever. Seeking signs of where and how to find the bread, the people had to be more amazed when Jesus announced: "I am the bread of life." (John 6:35) Faith is as easy as breathing in and out. Breathing in the experience of God and breathing out your witness for God. A daily life of breathing in and breathing out the reception of and sharing of the Holy One is the adventure of faith. I have chosen the daily bread of life grown by faith in Jesus Christ.

Thus, I pray the Lord's Prayer, the Apostle Creed, the prayer of David, the prayer of Jeremiah and personal prayers each morning throughout the weeks. I invite you to feed your soul. Don't try it; do it - read the Bible and talk to God. Come feast on the Word. Jesus is the bread of life. Gain strength for the living of these days on earth and manna for the eternal life. Praying in the name of Jesus is not a Burger King fast food experience by any means or stretch of the imagination, because it is not "a have it your way experience". It is a better way of experiencing immediate action; God hears and answers in a hurry: "Yes." "No." or "Wait." Do you believe?

I believe in God, I believe in Jesus Christ and I believe in the Holy Spirit. Come and enjoy the fruit of the spirit: love, joy, and peace. Come and enjoy the refreshing water and spiritually hydrate to the glory of God.

PRAYER: "Lord Jesus Christ, Son of God, grant mercy and healing upon us, who grieve. Amen."

Day 9

SAVING GRACE

Read: First Samuel 15

Manifestation of the unmerited favor of God is amazing. Think about it. Throughout salvation history favor is shown to people guilty of disobedience. God is "merciful and gracious, longsuffering and abounding in goodness and truth" (Exodus 34:6 NKJV) Where, oh where is this grace? It seems ridiculous in a world that seek punish upon punish. More and more, in the United States of America law enforcement officers are sought to be punished for the way they apprehend persons in violation of the law. Grace as the divine attribute of God bestows worth upon the worthless and deliver unmerited favor to the hopeless.

Paul instructed Titus in "saving grace." Titus does not have to work to receive the grace, but he works in response to the grace he has been given. The means of grace is there for Titus and all people, who come to believe in the acts of God as seen in Jesus the Christ. Titus is encouraged to "speak these things, exhort, and rebuke with all authority. Let no one despise you." (Titus 2:15 NKJV) Where am I to go to be taught such grace?

Saved by the grace of God though guilty of disobedience is unmerited favor. It is not news worthy to local or national or international newspapers. The quantity and quality of grace are immeasurable in that grace is unlimited. Amazing grace extended to murders, adulterers, thieves and others guilty of wrongs. The same grace extended to a pious and obedient servant is no less available to the respondent to offer favor from God. Divine is the love given to people and acceptable to believers. The realization of sin is challenging on earth, when the standards of ethics as set in Scripture are questionable or thought to be antiquated and molded and outdated. A beauty in being a believer is in knowing that through all the challenges there is qualitative mercy and patience with God.

A few hours following the reading of 1 Samuel 15 and Titus 3 and drinking delicious coffee, a jogging exercise made the beginning of our day as bright as ever. So, my "Wifie" and I decided to joy ride to a favored spot. Enjoying a peaceful drive, we reached the "Bridge" a connection between where we were to where we desired to be. Traffic was heavy as usual. Without an E-Z pass (prepaid token to cross the bridge) drivers made their way through the cash lane. Aggressive drivers were unmerciful and refuse to allow others to gracefully exchange positions. It appeared to be a mad race to pay the toll and keep traffic moving. People exchange shouts of frustration and derogatory signs. It was enough to send kind hearted persons into a shockwave, so my wife said: "Just let them go through." My driving gloves were not intended to be boxing gloves, so all of the ugly things said by aggressive drivers were met with silence.

On the other side of the bridge, we learned that a friend we hoped to see had been murder by weapons used to slice and dice him. No mercy or love was shown the "big guy." A few blocks from our spot of favor, a favored friend's blood was drying out on sidewalks which once were our pathway to church and parks and sundry matters of life. Through grief of losing our friend, thoughts of anger quickly change to sorrow knowing that in the end, it was a new beginning. Next to me was a wonderful person with whom the world is shared. Actualizing the essence of life changed thoughts from discourteous people and murders to capture present memories of past and enjoyment of the current. God's grace remains sufficient. The grace that brought Big Guy into the church five years prior to being murdered on the streets where only a few years before he had been "kingpin" and a non-believer. I recalled the day of his salvation, when he said: "Man, I want to learn like you and before I die have the right relationship with God. Man, I should have been dead and it is just a matter of time. Man, I tell you, Doc, I am going back to school and die a decent man." Where was I to find the grace of God, when our friend was murdered on a street in Harlem?

Grace is prevenient, known or unknown, received or rejected, accepted or denied; it is still grace. Grace is not "cheapen" by understanding. Grace has no reduction in value, but reveals transformative power, when human beings once unaware receive the awareness of grace. Such power cannot be minimized by cruelty and violence. Grace is a gift with no required reciprocity. Big Guy did graduate from college, doubling with a master degree and true to his word was entering a doctoral program to obtain the degrees that the first person to open a bank account for him had inspire him to do… A witness to his death took me to the actual spot and said: "As he was dying, we called for an ambulance. But he told me: 'It is okay. Thank God, I am saved.'" Where is saving grace?

"To whom much is given, much is required." Freeing grace requires reaction by human beings. God, the preeminent stockholder of grace, invest unlimited and unconditional love in human beings, so human beings as responsible recipients of grace may show grace. We do not disregard works. We work not for grace, but in response to the grace of God. Christians desire to be in obedience to God. Amazing grace was not in our non-reaction to the aggressive drivers that was just common sense and courtesy at best. Grace was the response of Big Guy believing in dying the death he envisioned would be, acknowledging that between 2005 and 2010 he had been set free to die that he might live. Grace, saving grace! May those who killed Big Guy, be grace to see the reception of their souls…there may grace be found.

Prayer: "Lord Jesus Christ, Son of God, grant mercy and healing upon us, who grieve. Amen."

Day 10

REMEMBERING A FRIEND

Read: Second Samuel 11

The hopes of many people departed this earth, when my friend died on October 25, 2009 at his home. In his local church, he was often viewed as a King David. The report went out that his last breath came as he was preparing to deliver his Sunday morning sermon.

A few months earlier in the year, I visited with him following a commencement ceremony. His driver was instructed to stop at a diner where we ate breakfast. It was my treat, since he was providing the transportation home. It had been a great day! The commencement ceremony was fitting. The fresh brewed coffee, bacon and eggs with homemade potatoes were delectable. The ride around the mountains was as exhilarating in the company of friends. He paid the driver to take him home first and wait, while we visited. He had few memoirs to show me before I was driven into the city.

My friend was a minister of the gospel not a football star, so my expectation was to see some treasured religious items. To my surprise, he was a huge golf fan, so displaying his latest memorabilia of his favorite player was his agenda. In my childhood, I was a fan of one athletic icon – a retired football star. To my amazement my friend was a friend of the superstar from my childhood. Laughing out loud, he took me over to his personal collections from his friend, who had captured my attention as the most impressive athlete of our life time. Well, on and on I spoke of the professional star, so my friend announced: "The next time he visits, we shall dine together." It was not to happen.

In the fall of the same year, I would interview as a guest on his television broadcast. He told his crew that the interview was one of the best he had ever produced. He urged me to view it. Mercy me, I never revisit personal interviews. I do recall how time flew as our like mindset discussed changing the world. We both had the unrelenting hope and faith that God could use such undeserving, but willing servants to transform lives and ultimately the world.

When we left the studio, we had our final talk. As we strolled down the avenue toward the train, he spoke of his great love for his wife. He laughed as he shared childhood memories of his children who brought him great fulfillment. I listened intently as he gave me encouragement going forth. His last words were: "Thanks for sharing your mind." I responded, "And thank you, Doc, for enriching ours." When I heard the news at midnight on October 2nd that he had left this world, I shook with sadness and a still silence came to my soul. A heart pacer that had recently been replaced had failed him. My friend slipped away in the night wind. On the weekend to follow, at his memorial services an enormous gathering of strangers came into commonality having in some sphere of time experienced life with our friend. We came to stand as a testament to the indelible handprint he had left in our lives. We remembered his amazing smile and love given righteously. His physical presence is missed on earth, but his soul soars for eternity.

Remembering a friend, a theologian, a preacher-pastor and brother-leader, too, I know that hope of meeting the star athlete may have died with him, but dreams of developing the ideal seminary for world peace and reconciliation are yet alive. In fact, our hopes are inflamed.

Strange in a brief moment in time imprints are left on hearts forever. In remembrance of the Ultimate Teacher - Jesus Christ, inspiration abounds to proclaim the "good news". Until the last breath is lifted from the body my soul occupies there shall be motivation to move from grief to the accomplishment of World Peace. Dried eyed and ready to live…a peacemaker is remembering a friend by carrying on the makings of peace.

PRAYER: "Lord Jesus Christ, Son of God, grant mercy and healing upon us, who grieve. Amen."

Day 11

METHODIST THEOLOGY

Read: First Kings 12

John Wesley taught a theology of grace. He wrote about salvation and the disciplines taught as means of grace toward entire salvation. What is "entire salvation" about, as if you could be partially saved?

Having never met a human being, who could give the ultimate reality of the entire understanding of God, John Wesley's teaching that entire salvation interest this inquire of journey incomplete until death. A theology of baseball is not the intention, but the illustration of a baseball diamond could be an object lesson. Being a fan of Major League Baseball what I'm about to do is a departure from my favoritism of Scripture alone to state a position from my Methodist roots... I coined a term: "METS THEOLOGY."

Imagine the bases in between two dugouts on the Divine playing field with the "good" home team in the right dugout and the "not so good" visitors occupying the left dugout. You are free to choose the team on which you are a player understanding your free agent status is annual. You could transfer to the other team as a matter of "free will." As for me and my house, we are with the home team.

You are not on one team or the other by virtue of creation. This is not a predestination schematic. Born into life and born again into living the life is a "heartwarming" experience. Some persons are privy to being bat boys or girls maturing and learning the game of life, before making a confirmation of faith in the home team.

This is not a spectator's playing time. The spectators are in the afterlife experience in the biblical view of "great cloud of witness", who may have once played their best on the same field of life.

Now, consider the diamond. Suffice it for now to label the bases on the Grace Field:

1. Prevenient Grace is the batter's box. This is the grace that sought us when we were still sinners.

    God's **prevenient grace** is with us from birth, preparing us for new life in Christ. "Prevenient" means "comes before." Wesley did not believe that humanity was totally "depraved" but rather God places a little spark of divine grace within us which enables us to recognize and accept God's justifying grace. Preparing grace is "free in all for all," as Wesley used to say.

2. Justifying Grace is first base. (Some might argue that it should be 2nd base.)

    Today some call God's **justifying grace** "conversion" or being "born again." When we experience God's justifying grace, we come into that new life in Christ. Wesley believed that people have freedom of choice. We are free to accept or reject God's justifying grace.

3. Regenerating Grace is second base. (Some might argue that it should be 1st base.)

    The Wesleyan argument would be that there no regeneration before new birth, so that regeneration follows being born again. The strangeness in the warming of the heart is life transforming by which in dying with Christ, believers are regenerated unto the new life with Christ.

4. Sanctifying Grace is third base.

    Wesley believed that, after we have accepted God's grace, we are to move on in God's **sustaining grace** toward perfection. Wesley believed the people could "fall from grace" or "backslide." We cannot just sit on our laurels, so to speak, and claim God's salvation and then do nothing. We are participants in what Wesley called "the means of grace" and continue to grow in Christian life.

5. Glorifying Grace is home plate. "Every knee shall bow and every tongue confess that Jesus Christ is Lord, to the glory of God the Father." (Philippians 2:5-11)

It is generally supposed, that repentance and faith are only the gate of religion; that they are necessary only at the beginning of our Christian course, when we are setting out in the way to the kingdom.... And this is undoubtedly true: there is repentance and faith necessary at the beginning; a repentance, which is a conviction of our utter sinfulness, guiltiness, and helplessness.... But, notwithstanding this, there is also a repentance and a faith (taking the words in another sense, a sense not quite the same, nor yet entirely different) which are requisite after we have "believed the gospel." Yea, this repentance and faith may necessary in every subsequent stage of our Christian course or we may not "run the race which is set before us." And this repentance and faith are necessary to our **continuance** and **growth** in grace, as the former faith and repentance were necessary to our **entering** into the kingdom of God.

While the goal of a home run is desirable, during grief remember that grace will be sufficient though you may strike out at times, keep stepping up to the plate striving to make it at least to first base…even a walk (mercy) to first base is good. Instantaneous salvation is possible and sometimes obtained, but most people will need help in making it home. So, please be patient. Keep the faith. Know that one day by the grace of God, a place at home will be obtained. Only believe!

PRAYER: "Lord Jesus Christ, Son of God, grant mercy and healing upon us, who grieve. Amen."

Day 12

YESTERDAY HAS GONE

Read: Second Kings 25

Anniversaries of marriage are null when the divorce is final. Dates of previous marriages are sent to the annuls. No amount of years, since that warm day of exchanging wedding vows may have meaning, once the judge declares it is final. The accumulations of material things are irrelevant to the one who stepped away. Within a day everything gained can be wiped away in a flash. Gone!

In 1977, a fire destroyed most of my belongings. Everything went up in smoke, except the clothing I wore, the car I drove and whatever was not left in the trailer. In the fire were jewelry, pictures, old coins, televisions, exercise equipment, etc. Yes, they were "gone with the wind." In the midst of the ashes there was a Bible that the fire burnt not one cover or page. Smoke surrounded the Word of God, but could not burn or destroy it. Even I was amazed!

More amazing today is the fact that yesterday is gone. In the wind there are things that have blown through the years. I guess you may say they are "gone with the wind." Yet, here is something from the teachings of Christ that can never be taken from us. It is like the Word of God in the midst of the flaming fire, protected through the rage. Salvation remains. Life granted by the gracious act of God in Christ is still mine, yours and indeed ours.

Sitting alone, I looked back on the yesterdays with visions of better days. Rest escaped me. There was a surge of life within speaking the urgency of now. Now is the time to live in the Spirit. Now is the time to discover the fullness of life. Now is the time to take hold of forever. Now is the time, when salvation remains to sustain, replenish and lead to rest.

Praying for new life, I found the answer and know God as the Provider. The answer is in living each moment receiving and stepping into the next gifts.

PRAYER: "Lord Jesus Christ, Son of God, grant mercy and healing upon us, who grieve. Amen."

Day 13

HOUSE OF PRAYER

Read: First Chronicles 17

I care not to remember everything about August 1st. That was the day my Papa (paternal grandfather) was carried to a cemetery on the outskirts of Orangeburg, South Carolina. The funeral service was too brief and the burial too short. There is nothing following the burial that I recall, but from the moment I walked up the stairs of Trinity Methodist Church in Orangeburg, South Carolina for the funeral service, my mind was focused on no one else except my "Papa." I had my own private ceremony that day. I do recall tuning in to hear "Will the Circle Be Unbroken" - Papa's favorite song. No one else mattered that day, not even my father and his crying sisters or my somber Granny Rouse. I am told that the preacher of the eulogy was Papa's friend and neighbor. I was nine years old and my best friend had died. I was determined not to cry on that day, because I promised Papa I would not cry. You see, on the day Papa died, there was a spiritual assurance inside of me that "Papa was okay; you are okay." Yes, call it whatever you may desire…I heard what I heard and since the hearing my tears have been dry and my faith has been water quenching the thirst of my soul. When we left Church, the undertaker's car seemed empty though full and in my mind Papa's favorite song filled private ceremony that day.

Papa's obituary mentioned churches he served, both AME and MEC. It mentioned the day he was converted, the day he was ordained, the day he married and it listed every son as well as daughters and even the in-laws. It spoke of Granny, his loving and devoted wife but never mentioned me, his grandson. It even said he was known for his spiritual and fervent messages generosity. I could attest to all of it but it never mentioned me. That was it! I was devastated. What was wrong with them? Did they not know that I was Papa's best friend…his "Boy?" Our parents and grandparents were good about loving us all and making sure we were all favored, but everyone knew how special I was to Papa. I was lost in the reality of the day. Papa was gone. Yet, forever close. One early morning, his grave and all my memories of him and the funeral cloud my thinking. Why? It is July. The last time I saw him alive was July 1964; when he lifted from his bed and cried out, "Boy, what are you doing here?" He was so excited that I was permitted into the hospital to see him. Those would be his last words spoken, I learned later in 1983. The male nursing assistant who was there to witness the special privilege granted to me a 9 year old grandson, lived two blocks from the parsonage during my tenure as pastor in his town. He recalled observing the event and how they were amazed that my grandfather spoke. Cancer had Papa in a coma, but he awakened just a moment for me and never again. I do not know the answer to my question of why? I do know this: I am glad I stayed in the House of Prayer tonight, because God hears us here and we may hear God, too.

PRAYER: "Lord Jesus Christ, Son of God, grant mercy and healing upon us, who grieve. Amen."

Day 14

WHAT IS THE MEANING OF LIFE?

Read: Second Chronicles 34

Discover the King of kings through the meaning of Matthew 1:18-25 as an establishment of the life work of Jesus in association with major figures and events in the history of Israel. Then, reflect on the life of your favorite celebrity in association with major entertainers and concerts in our historical times.

In the womb, Jesus was commissioned to save people from sins, manifest the presence of God, identify with the great King David, establish the role of the church, and model salvation glory.

There was humor spoken at the final service of the belated beloved finding the way to be a kid, while having to grow up early in life. Cute, too, was a statement of teasing about at least one star having entered the scene of stardom at an age much younger. Whatever, humorous or not, the reality seem to be that this life was gone too soon.

What does it mean to know your favorite person to ever live? The person, who amazed people with gifts, graces and talents and now has departed, so what thoughts come to mind? Theories of personality aside, life lived and life beyond death in the context of being known to some as "the greatest" simply hurts, right?

People may die and leave memories of brilliant performances, contributions and ways of orientating people into one world with one love for one people. Ethics must guide what "ought to be" concluded as the meaning of the life. In terms of civil rights, may it be right to conclude that your favorite contributor may represent the ideal of achieving what you conceive and believe. You, too, may become a model of planning and working hard. Just follow that star "no matter how hopeless, no matter how far" to reach the unreachable. Will you, will we?

Prayer: "Lord Jesus Christ, Son of God, grant mercy and healing upon us, who grieve. Amen."

Day 15

KEEP OBSERVANCE OF THE HOLY

Read: Ezra 6

The Holy Spirit ushered in new birth (Acts 2). A few followers of Christ, including eleven of the original twelve and the added one had a life changing encounter with the Holy Spirit. The experience gave life to the Christian church. The power of the Word brought in numerous converts on the same day from various cultures. They heard in their own language and in one sweep thousands joined the movement.

There are local churches having accounts of church growth. The Word is preached and soul winning is accomplished. The church grows by thousands. Still there are those with very little growth in numerical count, which are experiencing spiritual growth. The hope of the mission of Christ has always been to win souls.

The great commission sends believers into the world for the making of Disciples of Christ. The commission of bringing persons to Christ is not to be ignored. The need and purpose of the church is for growth in number of persons and spiritual development. John 6:54-69 is clear on the fact that some who become disciples will reject the teachings of Christ and refusing the Eucharist, while complaining in disbelief about the meaning of the Body of Christ. The Church is to be built on the confession of faith maintained by the faithful, who believe and know the Son of God.

The difference between leaving and staying is in believing. It is a believing in the fruit of the Holy Spirit as the authority as taught in Pauline theology. The Holy Spirit, alone, gives us the power to live in love. The only way to fulfill the will of God is to become love inspired, driven, and propelled. Without love, we are just religious people looking for physiological satisfaction to get our shout on - making noise. The fruit of the Spirit is the manifestation of love in joy, peace, long-suffering, kindness, goodness, faithfulness, gentleness, and self-control.

Through the experience of the Holy Spirit we become strong, secure, patient, orderly in conduct, good in character, humble and victorious.

Living in the Holy Spirit, remain constant in moving forth in the will of God. Have no fear of the law bring your all to the throne of God. Come and experience the life freeing gift of the fruit of the Holy Spirit.

Prayer: "Lord Jesus Christ, Son of God, grant mercy and healing upon us, who grieve. Amen."

Day 16

SPEAKING THE TRUTH

Read: Nehemiah 9

True is the fact that everyone needs somebody sometimes. There are women expecting the truth to be spoken by all within their intimate circle of friends. They would love to have everyone in the world tell the truth. As women mature, they learn even dearest friends may not always speak the truth.

People tend to be guarded. They guard their emotions and try to protect the emotions of friends. Many persons in the world want the truth, but crumble in it. Things go wrong, when we crumble. With every lie uncovered more truth is needed. It is not the truth of the matter of the lie that will heal and cure the issues caused by the lying. No. What is needed in the uncovering of a lie is the emotional truth and mental unveiling of thoughts. How do you feel? What do you think? When and how are you going to respond? Truth may not be gained from evidence of the past. Historical facts are like diapers on a baby; changed to clean up the necessary mess. The importance of truth is in the currency of the moment. Truth is to be found in the actuality of honesty bathed in righteousness on the spot.

While facts are to be ignored, personal assurance is in what is personally lived. Persons live the facts they are making. Walking by faith into revealed facts as lived by others' interpretation. The current moment requires speaking the truth, so that each moment of living carries with it the essentials of living in current realities. Women want the truth, while often withholding truth within. Speaking through silence is not the same as speaking in verbal voice. Male or female, the gender form is not the crutch to speaking the truth or lying. Integrity and godliness are not gender specific.

Feelings and thoughts are utilized to prevent hurt and pain. Human beings appearing to be passive may actually be loading guns for an aggressive attack. There are ways to prevent the onslaught of war. One way is through the intelligent means of education. Another is the so-called "The Intelligent Design." Whatever will get you there, take the leap of faith, and come to appreciate assertiveness over passive aggressiveness or aggression. Aggression is a detriment in the grief recovery process. Good anger is controlled anger that seeks not to harm another.

Christians are encouraged to follow the teachings of Christ, which has to do with doing unto others as you would have them do unto you. A person wanting the truth spoken must be willing to not only speak the truth to others, but has to be able to handle the truth spoken with the same love imparted. There is the matter of heart! Can people be honest with each other with sacrificial love? Sacrifice the need for facts and accept the need for honest relationships in the here and now.

Facts are needed for courtroom lawsuits. Love is needed for faithful relationships. May we receive the wisdom of counsel that enables us to speak truth without harm to others or to ourselves? May we have the serenity and courage necessary to accept the unchangeable and ability to change the changeable? The rule of thumb is to speak what is helpful, and flush the harmful. Speaking the truth requires love in being Christian.

Prayer: "Lord Jesus Christ, Son of God, grant mercy and healing upon us, who grieve. Amen."

Day 17

LIVING IN DENIAL, SAVED BY GRACE

Read: Esther 8

Likes of him, she thought, she would never meet. He had mastered the teachings of the Master Teacher and Redeemer. His words flowed with the truth of agape. It got her attention. She knew he was the one. So, she called him out.

He could not escape, but he could deny. He denied their relationship. Right there on the spot, he denied their relationship. A relationship so intimate; a relationship so divine; a relationship created and not made is what it was supposed to be. A relationship for the ages not just of the moment is what it was thought to be. He denied even knowing the One who had given life to his loins and new birth to his soul. Why?

What was the nature of his fear? What was there to fear losing? Oh, right, he would lose his right to speak of a relationship he denied? He would lose his work, and life occupation that soared beyond imagination from the power of the love he denied, right? He would lose his so-called friends or fellow ethnic buddies, whose love had already saved him, right? Or maybe he would lose his historic witness or his precious now or anticipated coming fame, right?

She called him out. Witnessed as being one of them by others, he still denied the greatest love of life. You may be vain enough to think this is about you. Are you? I admit, it sounds a lot like me. But it is not a story of you or me. Yet, it is the story of every Peter, who denied Jesus, the lover of our souls. Peter denied him. In denying his relationship with Jesus, Peter placed at risk his earthly life, and his soul. Human beings are risk takers, for sure. However, denial is not the end of the story for Peter, and may it not be for us.

True love forgives. In fact, true love warns us of our pending need to deny the relationship. True love even desires the denial for the sake of a purpose greater than our willingness to die. More important than affirming or confirming the earthly relationship is the need to give affirmation to the eternal relationship. No matter how much we love on earth, our love is finite. God, alone, is infinite. We are to live as we live for God.

That is right. We live as we live for God. In God is the one true and undeniable relationship. It is the one for which true love forgives, when our soul is at stake. We are too often living in denial. Thank God we are saved by grace. This grace undeserved is so divine.

Can you hear Peter? Can you hear me? Can you hear you saying: "Oh Love of my life, forgive my denial?" Can you hear love saying: "Forgiven, for you know not what you do?"

Saved by grace, living in denial! Living in denial, saved by grace!

Prayer: "Lord Jesus Christ, Son of God, grant mercy and healing upon us, who grieve. Amen."

Day 18

RESULTS OF BUILDING THE BODY OF CHRIST

Read: Job 42

Ephesians is known as the letter of the Apostle Paul to the church of Ephesus. Scholars disagree as to who really authored the words. Still we can rest assure that God had stake in it. Why? Because the ability to communicate is of God and the wisdom of the message is too divine to be human void of God.

I teach from Ephesians as the manual for building the body of Christ - The Church. So, the importance of the author is minimal to the importance of the message. The Christian Church is an institution birth at Pentecost, according to the New Testament Scripture. It is to be known as consisting of all regenerated souls, each redeemed by the Blood of Christ and transformed by the Holy Spirit. In Ephesians 5:25, we learn that Christ loved the Church, and gave his life for it. Why?

Yes, he died that the Church might become His Body on earth, which He heads from Heaven. As members of the Church, we are called out from the system of the world. We are called to be body builders for Christ. Strengthening the body of Christ yields results all may appreciate. We live for the making of the Kingdom of God on earth.

The results of building the body of Christ are:

1. Repentance. The Church was birthed, according to Acts 2:38, with Peter calling for persons to repent and become disciples in the Body of Christ.

2. Salvation. Regenerated persons coming by way of the new birth, Acts 2:47, added to the Church. Building the body of Christ yields new

members into the local churches, and increase number of saved souls in the world.

3.   Faith in the Lord Jesus Christ as Savior, Son of God, who has mercy and grace for the repenting soul.

4.   Baptism. We baptize in the tradition of the Trinity, Acts 2:38, as a means of grace for the acknowledgement of God's initiative in cleansing us from sin, ushering in justification and sanctification for righteous living.

5.   Love. Jesus said by this love you have for one another they will know you are my disciples, John 13:35 reminds us. In the 15th chapter of the Gospel of John, Jesus taught that the disciples who love as He loves are His friends. "What a friend we have in Jesus."

6.   Continuance. In accord with Acts 2:42, a final result of building the Body of Christ is the recycling of the doctrines. We teach each to reach each. Each generation is to be taught to reach each soul of their day, and baptize in the name of the Father, Son, and Holy Ghost from Jerusalem to Samaria to Judea unto the uttermost parts of the world.

There is it. Our exercise in the Spiritual Fitness Center is to turn around from bad habits unto good living. Soaking in the fountain of life, lifting one another, and caring for the soul of all, we march on teaching the love of Christ by faith hoping for a better world on earth as it is in heaven. I have it! Do you?

Prayer: "Lord Jesus Christ, Son of God, grant mercy and healing upon us, who grieve. Amen."

Day 19

PREPARING THE WAY

Read: Psalm 100

It is a gift to have a profile of characters and be able to call one up from within at the drop of a dime. The characters may have meaningful and modernize some valid points of Scripture. They could often be home runs in speaking to the youth of the day. In fact, the inner child of most adults may come to life, when identifying with a character from a gifted presenter. Characters may become hits for evangelizing and healing human hearts.

Characters designed to reach into the heart and soul of the hearers in the midst of grief may be console and comfort. Driving home the point of a homily on Scripture or sometimes preparing the way for a sermon on grief could help many in the healing process. Interesting how God intervenes in prayer to prepare the way to the cross.

Often the crosses of life experiences are to be viewed, before a person can determine the relevance of the Cross of Calvary. Persons are facing the crosses of discouraging, disappointing, and damaging matters of growing up in changing times. Issues of molestation, parental abuse, peer pressure, etcetera, while needing to hear a call to come to Jesus. Jesus, who has been waiting for all to come as we are. "PREPARING THE WAY" for a life with Christ can be moving from the variety of characters within to the Character of God at the core within the Kingdom of God.

The validity of the Christian mission is not to be found in human decisions to hold on to flaw characters. The mission of Christ should always be known by the decision that God made and we should follow every step of the way. It is the decision that men and women, boys and girls are to be followers of Christ and baptized in the name of the Father, Son, and Holy Ghost. Salvation is about coming to Christ. Salvation has nothing to do with having our way, because God is not Burger King, but Jesus is the Prince of peace. Is it our mission? No, it is the Christian mission that guides the moments in existential proclamation of the Resurrected Lord Jesus Christ, who lives and reigns forever.

A Christian decision does not stop the power of hope in the characters within and characters shall not hinder the faith-sharing from within. We march forth as Christian soldiers not by personal orders. No, no! We press on toward the mark of the higher calling, because we have always done it for one reason alone - we are "preparing the way" for those to come and give their lives to Jesus Christ, the only Savior.

Prayer: "Lord Jesus Christ, Son of God, grant mercy and healing upon us, who grieve. Amen."

Day 20

REDEMPTIVE LOVE

Read: Proverbs 31

Community health projects may have a three-fold perspective with awareness from the medical community, faith community and community based organizations. Annually coalitions may hold massive health fairs. It is a day of redemptive love! A day of hope!

The annual event may be purposed for addressing health disparities among people of various ethnicities. Ethnic groups have been documented as being disadvantaged in prevention and treatment of particular maladies, such as diabetes, hypertension, obesity, etc. Equal treatment in light of ethnicity is a social reality that requires 21st century priority in health care and pastoral care. A large city may be a multicultural magnet for the world and it is necessary that to redeem people who have been neglected and abused in health care services. People with all backgrounds: race, religion, age, sexual orientation, class, immigration status, veterans and others with disabilities are in need of equality in care giving. What shall be done?

Children of Israel, we discover in the book of Exodus, were redeemed by the power of love. They were liberated from Egypt and brought through the Red Sea, because agreements were fulfilled in spite of difficulties. The illnesses and natural disasters that rocked Egypt passed over the people of faith, so that they were led beyond the sea of challenge to become a covenant people of God. Today, we are challenged to cross the sea of ethnicity into a wilderness of family diversities. Personalities of various cultures bring a pleasant uniting force of compassion for their respective professions and people of the world. Such love is redemptive. It is not to be known by sources of discrimination, but positive associations.

The positive associations are producing acts of kindness that may be duplicated around the world. People are starting in their own backyard as to be free from discrimination and prejudice behaviors by the power of redemptive love. You are invited to join in this movement of redemption. Death and dying has no greater champion of Life and living, which is to the delight of loving mothers.

Prayer: "Lord Jesus Christ, Son of God, grant mercy and healing upon us, who grieve. Amen."

Day 21

"EYE: 'I'"

Read: Ecclesiastes 12

On a "Community Walk" we stopped to enter a local historical tourist promotion company, and inside is embedded on the wall, the world's shortest poem written by Muhammad Ali, the famous United States of America's former heavyweight champion of boxing. Ali authored: "Me: We." How profound? I was reminded of our visit, when I asked my assistant to interpret my poem titled "Eye" with only a one word content - "I." I warned that it was based on my existential philosophical anxiety with the here and now. In the making of all interpretations comes down to what the "I," the person thinks.

Now, I wrote this to my assistant: "Here is my philosophy of this week found in the content of my poem titled, 'Eye: I' and I would like for you, as hearer of my existential anxiety, to decipher my depth of meaning."

Three hours later the response came: "It sounds like Ali's 'Me: We' poem but 'Eye: I' makes me think of our 'third eye,' being the spirit and soul truly being and seeing who we are."

So on point! I went on to give the original thought that led to "Eye." I went on to write, "Interesting and dynamic! You just rewrote or wrote a new version, because my content was only 'I,' but I named it 'Eye' in that the original meaning has to do with 'all ever seen' in a person, called I. Therefore, the I of each of us is examined. Yes, you are right, it's the human eyes and the eye of the soul looking at 'I.'" Continuing I wrote: "I like that you recalled Ali's 'Me: We.'"

Ali's thought was simple, though very profound. He believed that as the "Me" becomes "We" - We become One. Ali's early life and the successes he made was all about him becoming who he was destined to become, however, the more he became, the more the ME became WE as the world joined in with him and unified to become ONE, which was ideally his hope, for the world to become, in its truest sense, ONE nation under God.

For me, it is the "I" discovered in your mirror, and in your soul? This time the soul is mine:

1. Compassionate communication is essential to effective pastoral care in sincere ministry. Marion's death is an example. Marion is a small town in South Carolina. Life witnessed in Marion holds positive and negative experiences. My parents who met in Marion to begin their life together are buried in Marion marking the ending of their life on earth. During the death and dying experience of our parents, the local pastor was more than a key, he was essential through it all. The ministry of sincere caring and empathizing gave assurance, especially as our Mother transitioned that "though she died, yet shall she live." The human body met the cessation of life, but her soul was believed to be acceptable to the Infinite One - God. Death may be one of the worst times, even when loved ones appear ready to die and cross over the threshold of eternity. Compassionate communication requires the art of listening and caring, while being there. The pastor did not assume that a family filled with clergy would not need the strength of his pastoral care. What the minister gave was a sincere ministry of respect that the live lost was heartfelt and mental agony.

2. Respectful closeness with the touch of love. God's love is comforting. Pastor care in the most sincere form is supportive and respectful of people. Human touch offered in the right manner eases pain. Avoidance of persons in their lost may leave them void of godly presence. Void of persons entering the space of vulnerability could cause avoidance of acceptance of the reality of life beyond death. People in the midst of pain should have pastoral care. The touch of empathy may be assuring. A touch that speaks volumes about care gives meaning in silent voice. Reaching out with touch in times of grief may yield empathetic love at its best.

3. A time to cry in pastoral care is a time of allowing tears to speak truth of feelings and thoughts. Crying can be an eraser of the worst feeling and thoughts as it cleanse the soul of pain within. It may be healthy to cry in the safety of empathetic people. Crying without shame or undue stress, it may help in monitoring the grief process in the comfort zone of persons who care. I have been there. After delivering a eulogy of my mother and ten months later my father the experience of tears flowing was met with

acceptance by sincere hearts of people caring with me. The tears of a pastor rendered the message of sincerity of heart, which not only eased some of the pain it erased the shame associated with men crying. I had lost parents and I did not like it. So, I cried until crying erased the pain.

4. Acceptance of the reality of time is an art form in pastoral care. All things in time. Ecclesiastes gives a summary to time in the third chapter of the Old Testament text. It reveals a time to be born, a time to love, a time to plant, a time to sew, a time to build up, a time to war, a time to die ... a time of peace, a time to weep ... a time to mourn, a time to embrace ... a time to laugh ... a time to dance. Marion holds memories of life and death. Marion holds time, which once moved too fast, still now. Time has moved from my June 22nd birth in 1955 through the years, but with a permanent stillness in Marion, which says on April 15, 2002 and again February 19, 2003 time stood still for Lula W. Rouse and Bishop C. Rouse, respectively, and with them a part of me stands still in the reality of the times in Marion.

Thus, in essence, the term "I" is the great "I AM." Let those who have the "Eye" to see, seek the understanding through the guidance of the Holy Spirit. Pray! This is written to encourage you to come to know who you are through prayer. It is written that the eye in your soul may discover God in the discovery of knowing the "I" in your identity. In this life, we shall surrender freedom of our will to the guidance of God, who knows us as we are and how we ought to be. In so knowing, we know life beyond death. We begin to know we are infinite inside the great I AM, THAT I AM. I pray, we will.

Prayer: "Lord Jesus Christ, Son of God, grant mercy and healing upon us, who grieve. Amen."

Day 22

LOVE: AN ETHICAL DECISION

Read: Song of Solomon

John Wesley is known as a founder of the Methodist Movement in search of the Scriptural way of salvation and a life of holiness. A member of the holy club at Oxford in the 18th Century, he studied in the tradition of piety seeking inner peace and divine grace. His search established the foundation of a world-wide parish promoting Christian Perfection, a doctrine of perfected love. It comes home to me, because I am vowed to be a Methodist from birth until death.

In appreciation of the historical and theological experiences of life, the kinship with other faith groups is a hopeful experience.

A ministry of reconciliation grew into focus for me at the age of five in Hartsville, SC and crystallized at the age of sixteen in Kingstree, SC. The intentional ministry of reconciliation is a peace movement. It is a movement for the establishment and maintenance of world peace, which I shall live unto death and then.... It is not new with my calling. With every paradigm shift worth following is the core essentiality of the will of God. Seek to know the will of God for your life and be assured that though we die, yet shall we live.

What is the will of God for your life? Discover the will of God and abide in the intentional peace movement, so as to build on a solid foundation of love, peace and joy. Live until death; then live forever in peace. It is an ethical choice.

Prayer: "Lord Jesus Christ, Son of God, grant mercy and healing upon us, who grieve. Amen."

Day 23

In The Morning, When I Rise

Read: Isaiah 53

Early in the morning, when I would rise, I could smell the sausage or hear the bacon popping or count on having honey-baked ham with scrambled eggs and buttermilk pancakes or biscuits covered in syrup being served with love. Mother's breakfast was a homecoming feast. I enjoyed her cooking. It was food sopping good.

Early the first day of the week, Mary Magdalene and the other Mary went to dress the crucified body of Jesus within the tomb. Behold! What followed the disruption of the earth at the murder of Jesus was an angelic presentation of love. God had cooked up a homecoming feast for his favored. Jesus had arisen from the grave. Oh, what a morning, when the sun returned to shine. He lives!

Easter forever reminds me that as sure as there is death, there is a blessed assurance of resurrection. At the point of death, I have thought there was no chance of life. The death of love; the death of relations; the death of dreams; death and death; all manners of death have pain and challenges the assurance of eternity. How many times have human beings found reality in the on again-off again love stories. We, too often, live soap opera lives. What's your story line?

In the end, when all comes to rest, and only one resurrection remains - give me Jesus. When my eyes roll back and life on earth ceases to be; give me Jesus. When the sun refuses to shine for me and night seems my eternity; give me Jesus. In the afterlife, may there be a morning light and in that morning when I rise, give me Jesus. Why?

Because Jesus is more than a historical figure teaching and preaching, He is the faith experience of God's deliverance from death into everlasting life. Living the Jesus experience, my entire life is in the eternal assurance of life beyond death. The value of living to die from sin, so as to live again forever in the glory of salvation is the greatest satisfaction of life. The entire salvation experience consummates at the end of the faith adventure.

Thus, you are invited to accept the eternal life known to be real and life sustaining; Come to believe Jesus!

Prayer: "Lord Jesus Christ, Son of God, grant mercy and healing upon us, who grieve. Amen."

Day 24

DEITY OF CHRIST

Read: Jeremiah 31

Who is Jesus of Nazareth? He is known to some people as a human being who came with three offices: prophet, priest, and king. They speak of him as teacher, savior, and ruler of the universe. What do you say of Jesus?

In Christian evangelical culture, Jesus is the primary source of the faith experience of God. He is the source of our communicating from one searcher to another God's incarnation. Hungering for the manna of God, persons look to Jesus for spiritual feasting on the Word. In this sense, Jesus is the Biblical personality that central to an understanding of God in humanity. He is not the current existential experience of God, yet the primary source for our understanding the experience of God in existence, here and now with anticipation of life beyond this space in time. Jesus is the assurance of eternity.

How do you know Jesus of Nazareth? Answers to the following questions will measure your understanding of Jesus Christ.

1. Have you studied the entire Bible, Old and New Testaments? Study the entire Bible, then you will know Jesus of Nazareth.

2. When was the last time you read through the Bible in accordance with suggested Scriptural readings? Structured daily reading of the Bible is a roadmap to knowing Jesus of Nazareth.

3. Is Jesus Christ at the center of your life? Describe the centering of your life focused on God. If you are centered on Christ, write a story on your experience of Jesus.

4.   Have you been baptized into the Christian faith or reaffirmed your baptism within the last two years? How is baptism a means of grace in the experience God?

5.   What is the most glorious event to happen in your life? What is the meaning of salvation found in the sacrificial life of Jesus?

The means of grace in understanding Jesus Christ is through correct study of the Bible. It is not the only means of grace. Revealed within the Bible are the sacramental means of Baptism and Holy Communion through which may be found the mysterious tremendous experience of God. The Gospel of Mark provides the prophetic role of Jesus of Nazareth, who came to teach with authority. There is truth found in knowing Jesus has life transforming teachings. The deity of Christ is experienced by way of Holy Baptism and Holy Communion, which having been instituted by Jesus Christ, signifies to the world the reign of Christ in the life of believers. Only God can so teach an unlearned like me - He rules!

Prayer: "Lord Jesus Christ, Son of God, grant mercy and healing upon us, who grieve. Amen."

Day 25

DIVINE SILENCE

Read: Lamentations 3

In a time of stillness! Divine silence is to be treasured. During such time, hear the unheard.

Traveling a days' journey by car, I returned to teach at the seminary. I had moved on December 1, 2003 proximately 1,200 miles from the school. In the classroom there was no television or radio. We did not have a guest artist or professional entertainer. No one carried on conversation to disrupt the teaching process. In fact, silence fell upon the theological students and we listened to hear a word from God. I had prepared to teach, but to precede God, so I requested stillness in the silence. I did not ask for silent prayer, but silence. It was a time of just listening. Then, ending the period of silence, students reported having heard the wind outside, cars passing by, other students beyond the doors talking, and even the whistling of another professor. Not one person reported hearing God, so we went into silent prayer.

The difference was in a time of silence, the focus was on listening. Everyone was asked to be in silence and after a period of time speak to what they heard during the time of silence. However, reflecting on the time of silent prayer, everyone had something to say about speaking to God or what they heard from the Lord, during their time of praying in silence. On that day "divine silence" was born in my mind and soaked my soul. Divine silence is time spent listening to God, but more than hearing it is also a time to be heard. Divine silence has become a time for clarity of mind - moments of open heart and soul searching before coming out with critical reflection – theology on divine silence.

Hearing God! Believing and living into what we have heard. The Divine to human relationship fuels our actions for the coming days, weeks, months and through the years. Believing what is heard is of God believers do, speak, and live out of the experience of divine silence into spiritual disciplined lives. It has been said: "Actions speak louder than words." Actions in our lives are influenced by authoritative teachings heard during the divine silence, which guides our living and sustains us even through the experience of death and dying. Pray in the still of the night and listen as God speaks through the silence.

Prayer: "Lord Jesus Christ, Son of God, grant mercy and healing upon us, who grieve. Amen."

Day 26

THE ABUNDANT LIFE

Read: Ezekiel 37

Abundant life yields witness to the love of God. It is directed by the Holy Spirit amidst human circumstances. Grounded in the belief in Jesus as the Christ, the abundance of life is more than victory over physical death; it is living victoriously over human conditions: poverty, illnesses, death, etc. Christians walk by faith, not by sight. Therefore, Christians ought to have a daily deportment reflecting victory in every situation. Difficult at times cannot defeat believers, because of faith in God's deliverance.

Our children were encouraged to live the abundant life. While, I would not label it "street theology", it was akin to the radical theology of love highlighted in the living of Martin Luther King, Jr. So, it may be termed a heart theology. In a heart of godliness there abides compassion for lives.

In 1985, our children desired to have a ministry to persons with HIV/AIDS; challenged me as to why I was not a pastor in a church with Blacks and Whites (all God's people); and vowed to give monies beyond their needs to the poor. Tears pouring from their faces, and most if not every challenge they proposed met, they asked their cognitive processing father to remember the emotions of the heart. "People should be respected for what they feel. There is no place for discounting and devaluing the emotions felt in children. Parents need to awaken to thinking about what it may feel like to tell a child you do not care about their feelings. God is not telling us to 'just get over it.' God cares too much to ask you to place your mind over your heart and get on with it. God offers us grace to merge the feelings of the heart with the wisdom of the mind, so that we keep the faith while hoping in the future. It is with this faith that we work on through the tears with our eyes on the prize."

I confess, in my mind, I only know Jesus as the way, the truth, and the light. Yet, in my heart, I want to be like Jesus. I want to live life in such abundance that I give as the Good Samaritan or the woman at the well or Peter and Paul or a generous star athlete or unto death as many have done before. I want to give as Jesus gave life for the life of all. My mind says, "No," but my heart transforms my mind into a heavenly chorus that sings: "Lord, I want to be like Jesus, in my heart." Medger Evers, Martin Luther King, Jr, James Chaney, and many more gave their lives for us. "Lord, I want to be like Jesus, in my heart." Preachers, teachers and other leaders place their lives on the line for us. Lord, I want as your child, who cares with filled hearts of abundant love. Oh, to be like Jesus. Before I come to die, I shall give abundantly.

Prayer: "Lord Jesus Christ, Son of God, grant mercy and healing upon us, who grieve. Amen."

Day 27

WHERE SHALL WE BEGIN...

Read: Daniel 9

Begin each year seeking an understanding of God. God in the tri-personal nature: Father, Son, and Holy Spirit are the three distinctive persons of our God. The only God, who is above all and in all, is with us. Emmanuel!

We speak of the invisible Godhead as the Father. God has literally not been seen by human eyes. Only one exception is declared challenging this belief, so as to speak that in the Son, Jesus, our Lord, who as spoken of in John 1:18 abided in the bosom of the Father.

Jesus is viewed as the Son of God, and is in all the fullness of the Father manifested in the flesh. Many have come to understand by faith the oneness of the Triune God, which we have been centuries removed from as human beings. The Holy Scriptures gives witness through the teachings of Jesus that the Son was the existence of God in humanity. Jesus was human, yet divine being one with God as the Incarnation of God in the flesh.

The Holy Spirit is the realization of God acting upon believers and convicting human beings of sin, while guiding the believer into all truth. So today, we shall begin with the reception of the Holy Spirit – God as the Source of our deliverance through the valley of the shadow of death. In good and bad times, God is in humanity. In the face of the death of persons close or distant or facing our personal pending cessation of life, search the Holy Spirit for the comforting presence of God.

The doctrine of the Trinity is revealed in the New Testament. Everyone can engage in the study of the Trinity. Through our studies in the bible each person may experience God in their own unique way.

Our years shall be filled with divine power, when we begin and end annually in search of God. In the beginning of the year, we experience the Father, Son, and Holy Spirit. In the end of each year, we know that through each cycle there is God – Alpha and Omega. We get to know God as Alpha and Omega, the Beginning and the End. Let us experience God through His Word and share the Agape with others that God shared with us through Christ!

Prayer: "Lord Jesus Christ, Son of God, grant mercy and healing upon us, who grieve. Amen."

Day 28

TIME BEYOND EXPECTATION

Read: Hosea 4

The humanity and feelings of Jesus are captured by the writer of the Gospel of Luke. There is joy in realizing that Jesus though divine understands the human condition. From the birth of Jesus through his three years of ministry, his experience on the Cross, his bursting through the grave and his heavenly ascension, people of faith are led to know him beyond expectations.

The Anointed One was expected to come and liberate the people of God through a militant takeover. The time beyond expectation reveals that his non-violent plan of action has defeated the betrayal and violent attack on his person. Strange as it remains, the willingness of Jesus to go to the cross and suffer in the hands of sinners for whom He would die is the greatest act of bravery ever shown.

Bee lives beyond expectations. She had it all thought out in her mind. A husband and children with a home untouchable by the principalities of the world; she would dance and sing through life with ease. It was a wish fulfilled until that awful day, when Lawrence drove away and by cell phone called the attorney requesting divorce. Why? Did he not expect the everlasting to be forevermore? Did he not expect their family of comfort to endure the trials of time?

When he came to my office to explain his actions before a tear driven Bee, he waded through the remorse to say: "Tell her love felt the need to leave her. Tell her love felt the need to free her." Words seemed honest enough. The pain within Bee gave a death ear to such unexpected communication and she sought to know the "who" beyond the explanation of Love's why.

"Who is she or they? How long has this been going on?" Without the answers to her questions, she had no expectations of making it another day. What is there beyond the perfect home and the best love ever known.

Forgiveness! It is about forgiving and seeing. We are past the Christ event and know that his words from the cross are of great significance. "Forgive them for they know not what they do." In human circumstances of separation and divorce, when odds bring life beyond what we expect living to be, we have to find the place of emotional forgiveness, which is often found after we make the conscious decision to forgive.

Without all the answers, one day she took the leap of faith. She decided to forgive and let go. In so doing, she let God take her to a place beyond it not being over now into a place of new beginnings. She no longer needed the sorrow of of another because she had the assurance of God. We have the victory in Jesus through the sufferings and disappointments.

When the sufferings and disappointments come beyond our control, make the conscious decision to overcome them with the bravery of leaping into the unexpected future saved by grace through faith. Believe this: Emmanuel - God is with you. The dance is no longer one of ease, but it is the best ever when you are dancing with the Lord of the dance. Come, Jesus has been waiting for you. Call on him!

Prayer: "Lord Jesus Christ, Son of God, grant mercy and healing upon us, who grieve. Amen."

Day 29

THE COMING OF THE LORD

Read: Joel 2

Subway preachers tend to have the same message. They urge everyone to repent and be saved, because Jesus is on His way back NOW. Consistency is not an issue in the preaching of our subway interrupters. Their messages are clear and concise, and they collect their own monies from one car to another and one train to another. They provide us with an age old message in a new age time.

The message is as old as the time of Jesus. Jesus said He would be coming back. The Parousia is an expectation of the Christian faith. Though old in time, the truth is new in time. Truth never grows old it is renewed in every generation. Truth is an ageless reality of God's revelation. It is respected until fulfilled. Even in fulfillment, truth is ageless throughout history. I truly believe, Jesus is coming back as Christ our Lord. I am not astute enough to calculate the second, minute, hour, day, week, month, year, etc. My walk is by faith, not insight of the actualities.

There is help and hope for those of us who dare to believe. The apostle Paul encourages us to wait on the Lord, and be of good courage. Believing in the resurrection of Jesus, believe also in the return of Jesus. The witnesses of the resurrection also heard the promise of the teachings. The teachings of the Christian faith hold to be doctrine the facts of the coming of Jesus Christ. So, the subway intruders, who preach for the money on the daily, are not far from the truth - just incomplete in telling the whole truth. I have yet to hear our subway preachers speak to those who have preceded us in crossing from this life into eternal rest.

What happens to my paternal and maternal grandparents, my parents, my uncles and aunts and other relatives and friends, who have gone from here to there? Wherever there may be, when I call their names they may hear me but I dare not to hear them. Granny Rouse was 97 years old. She outlived my grandfather and all of her children, except one. She has witnessed the departure from this life of a grandchild and great-grandchild. A host of relatives and friends have gone where she has now gone. Through all of life and the departure from this life unto the next her deep grounding in a faith held to the teaching that at the coming of Jesus Christ, the dead in Christ will arise first. Then, those who have been left behind yet alive will be caught up in the clouds together with them and be with the Lord forever. What happens?

An eternal party is what happens? The coming of the Lord is ushering in an eternal party. The message of "repent and believe" is incomplete without the entire gospel. The good news has to do with our defeat of death. The good news is that we are Easter people and there is a resurrection. The good news is that party time is coming! The Lord is on His way. So, at the coming of the Lord, we will leave this dress rehearsal to enjoy the real celebration. The invitations have been handed out, sealed with the blood of Christ! We wait patiently for the host! Come, Lord Jesus, come!

Prayer: "Lord Jesus Christ, Son of God, grant mercy and healing upon us, who grieve. Amen."

Day 30

EVANGELISM

Read: Amos 9

Pastors of congregations who seek to increase the kingdom of God here on earth by prayerfully reaching out to everyone may encounter needs beyond physical concerns. In fact, the saving grace of God may be needed spiritually for human souls. Our desirable outcomes are:

1. Encouraging the leadership in every local church within their areas to work with pastors to carry out the mission of Jesus Christ to make disciples.

2. Equipping clergy and laity in the area with more tools for the work of evangelizing in urban ministry, as well as rural ministry.

3. Evangelizing with a mission to grow the church membership numerically through strong leadership, dynamic worship, committed stewardship, faithful discipleship, and participatory fellowship.

4. Enlarging the target areas of the local churches in their areas through partnerships in ministries, and cooperative witnessing for membership growth.

What is evangelism? A leader placed emphasis on definitions for evangelism born out of the nature of the Christian mission. In essence, everything done for Jesus Christ is evangelizing, when the desirable outcome is the "making of disciples of Christ."

Evangelism has always been the FLAGSHIP of winning souls, when such is bringing persons into commitment to the Christian faith. It is a bold step in the right direction for evangelism by adding to the local church (denominational) membership vows. Persons joining local churches should vow to "uphold the local church by your presence, prayers, service, gifts, and **witness**." The primary call of Jesus is to make disciples under the authority of the Holy Spirit.

The church is not a playground of secular ideas and activities. Church is a place for spiritual grounding in sacred ideals and formations. Secularism seeks relationships and memberships, because the very nature is to form social clubs. Spiritualism in the Christian faith has to do with **worship, discipleship, fellowship, leadership, and stewardship**, which has as its outcome reconciliation leading to sacred relationships and memberships as by-products of the mission not the primary purpose. Turning our mindset from secular thinking and to the spiritual disciplines, we will grow the local churches through the primary task of making disciples of Jesus Christ. Churches witnessing increase in members for the right reason are speaking convincingly, rebuking naysayers, encouraging the faithful and teaching with patience the seekers of eternity with God. People are dying and need the answer for eternal life – Jesus.

FLAGSHIP EVANGELISM

1. **Worship**
   1. **Praise**
   2. **Prayer**

2. **Leadership**
   1. **Convincing**
   2. **Concise**

3. **Stewardship**
   1. **Time**
   2. **Talents**
   3. **Treasures**

4. **Discipleship**
   1. **Missions**
   2. **Ministries**

5. **Fellowship**
   1. **Encourage**
   2. **Enrich**

6. Reconciliation
   1. Relationship
      1. Renew
      2. Rebuke by speaking the truth in love
   2. Membership
      1. Evangelize
         1. Witness
      2. Endure
         1. Working for Christ

Serving the Lord, until we die and then...

Prayer: "Lord Jesus Christ, Son of God, grant mercy and healing upon us, who grieve. Amen."

Day 31

LET THERE BE PEACE!

Read: Obadiah 10 & 21

I wonder: Whatever happened to singing of *"Let There Be Peace on Earth?"*

Where is the peace that was meant to be for the future good of the world? Really, where is the peace with justice? It was to begin with the person in the mirror. What happened? Perhaps the mirror cracked, right?

People come to church desirous of a place of peace. The place where people may come broken-down and wounded, unfit to live and receive the training in spiritual formation that fits them for the world. The church should be the place of *shalom*. The church of ordinary people is an extraordinary place. The Body of Christ is extraordinary and exists for the comforting of ordinary people. It is the place of worship.

In accordance with the teachings of Paul, the spiritual place of worship is individual and corporate oriented. The intentional giving of self to God daily with a commitment to corporate worship as a means of grace in helping others become fit for daily living in the Christian context. So pronounced are words I heard spoken in the past: **"The entire existence of believers should be sacrificial worship of God, in response to the sacrifice of God's Son (3:24-26). This requires choosing to be *transformed* in the mind by the Spirit of God (8:14; 1 Corinthians 2:12) rather than conforming to 'what everyone else does.'"**

Come dwell in a place of peace. Each day, when you awake, give thanks to God and clothe yourself in the study of the Bible. Wear righteousness as your garment of protection by living in holiness. Be an intentional maker of peace throughout each day, until it is unintentionally habitual. Memorize Scriptural verses every morning, so as to be equipped against the challenges of evil. Shield yourself from the temptations by standing firm in the faith. Know without doubt that you are saved by grace, which is efficiently sufficient. Pray in the spirit of asking God for all things good.

When we all carry the daily deportment of children of God, then will "peace be to the brethren, and love with faith, from God the Father and the Lord Jesus Christ." (Ephesians 6:23 NKJV)

Prayer: "Lord Jesus Christ, Son of God, grant mercy and healing upon us, who grieve. Amen."

Day 32

COMFORT ONE ANOTHER

Read: Jonah 3

In Jonah we are given a message indicating that the word of the Lord came to him a second time, instructing him to stop his doings and go to Nineveh. Why go to the great city of Nineveh and proclaim the word of the Lord? Jonah walked to the city and entered crying out that in 40 days the city would be overthrown. Then, the people of the city responded in belief by fasting and wearing sackcloth. God heard them in their acts of repentance and changed His mind regarding the destruction and bought no harm to them. The people of Nineveh came to divine silence and listened. They were not so busy or so loud as not to hear the word of God from one, who traveled from miles away to bring the message from The Divine, who requires at times divine silence.

Hello people! There is no relevance in questioning the return of Jesus Christ in the Christian context. Jesus is coming back! Yes, He is coming. We are not sure of when, where, or how. The fact of faith is that the Lord is coming and on His return those who are asleep in Jesus will see the Lord, before those yet alive, when He comes. Yes, He is coming back.

Rebecca died on Sunday, August 31, 2008! When persons die in our community of faith, the minister turns to the Bible for words of comfort. Sometimes those words come easy. There are times when words of comfort are difficult to find. In the case of Rebecca, the Word jumped into my mind without opening the Bible. Easy, I would say! Not amazed? Well, check this out. I did not know her. And, I do not know her life at this moment. I cannot tell you the numbers of years, months, weeks, days, etc. of her life. Nothing has been presented to me to say the number of moons and sunrises or sunsets she saw. Yet, the Word of God for her service came easy.

Paul in his elderly state of life wrote to churches, which embodied people that he loved. He left with them through writings his theological believes and wishes for the children of God. In one of his messages to the church of the Thessalonians, Paul encourages them to love one another and those beyond their city, in a city like this one having major Jewish influence and people worshipping various gods in the midst of the existence of God. Boldly the champion for the cause of Christ asked that those yet alive believe in the second coming of Jesus. By so believing, increase in your love of all people, strive to live in peace as you mind your own business, work and walk right, and be just toward others as you prosper in life. What a message!

The comfort to be found in the death of Rebecca or a loved one is in the message they leave. The comfort may be found in the message from their experience of time on earth. A message that reflects love above hate, peace to replace war, self-reflections as opposed to false accusations, an attitude of do unto others as you would have them do unto you, so that you prosper without harm to another soul. What is the message of Rebecca? It is a simple one. How do I know? I have just told you. Her message jumped right into my mind as though her spirit placed it there. Ready? It is real simple, because she died as she lived - in comfort. Her message is this: "Comfort one another!"

Prayer: "Lord Jesus Christ, Son of God, grant mercy and healing upon us, who grieve. Amen."

Day 33

AN ABUNDANT LIFE CENTER

Read: Micah 6, 7

The body of Christ is to be strengthened, built, and made whole within an abundant life center (Howard Clinebell). Christians are body builders for Christ, who worship for the most part within walls of facilities called churches. A church is most effective when body builders for Christ are providing abundant life ministries within and without the walls of the facility.

One such ministry is pastoral care. Pastoral care as a means of grace may be effective in healing and equipping body builders for *life in all its fullness.* Many churches are implementing various ministries through various aspects of pastoral care, one of which is pastoral counseling.

As a Licensed Marriage and Family Therapist and Fellow in the American Association of Pastoral Counselors, I acknowledge the reality of being a "wounded healer." (Henri Nouwen) My brokenness in human relationships has been as great as any human could face, even greater. In the same life, my connectedness with God is solid, and unsurpassed in human life. It is my unbroken faith and love in God that assures me daily of the future good for which I hope. Through therapeutic sessions the factors of healing and support are shared with others for their mental health and spiritual development.

Therefore, encourage the leadership team in your churches to develop an abundant life center for your congregation and community. Psychic, mental, spiritual, and emotional factors in human well-being can guide your theological ethos. How do we obtain, sustain and maintain goodness in human relations? Pastoral care and counseling is a means of grace by which the will of God for human relations may be sought.

Desirable outcomes of an abundant life center (Clinebell):

1. To liberate, empower, and nurture wholeness centered in the Spirit;

2. To foster spiritual formation and ethical guidance in human lives;

3. To utilize and integrate both psychological and theological insights regarding the human situation, and the healing of persons;

4. To be holistic, seeking to enable healing and growth in all dimensions of human wholeness;

5. To nurture wholeness at each stage of the life journey;

6. To effect a reparative ministry of pastoral counseling;

7. To develop a shared ministry of care-giving with the pastor and the whole congregation;

8. To develop short term crisis intervention methods;

9. To become trans-cultural in ministries of the local church;

10. To enable people to increase the constructiveness of their behavior as well as their feelings, attitudes, and values is crucial in the helping process;

11. To utilize the unique professional identity and role of ministers;

12. To use intuitive, metaphoric, imaging approaches integrated with analytical, rational, intentional, and problem solving approaches in whole person transformation;

13. To become more effective in liberating wholeness in both men and women;

14. To provide growth-oriented psychotherapies;

15. To provide pastoral care in all the diverse functions of ministries, including preaching, worship, and social action;

16. To be effective growth-nurturer. (Therefore, the congregation is encouraged to support the continuing education of the entire staff)

Prayer: "Lord Jesus Christ, Son of God, grant mercy and healing upon us, who grieve. Amen."

Day 34

PLAN THE WORK AND
WORK THE PLAN

Read: Nahum 1

Marie is an outstanding school teacher. She places insights into the minds of young people. The retention rate of her children is high. Each improve in their skills above the next grade level of expectation and excel in their required standardized texts. Ask the students why they learn from Ms. Marie and they will tell you: "She is a good teacher" and "we love her…" because she loves us," you will hear them gladly say. Ask the same question of Marie and you come away knowing rules of faith.

Marie is a Christian, who begins each day in prayer. She knows to pray. She is aware of others who pray for her, so that she is never alone. She accepts and understands the love of God. She is loved by her Christian leader, family members, colleagues, students and their parents. She walks in the assurance of being loved with the hope of her students' success. Each student receives what she teaches and gives back in the best of their knowledge.

Existence requires a walk of faith. A good walker understands that there are rules to follow on the journey. While learning to walk and jog in my youth, my parents encouraged me to pray, exercise and warm up my body eating healthy before taking off on the pathway to school. I continue the routine today on the pathway of life. Looking back over the years, 18 years beyond mid-life as promised, I note that good teachers, such as Marie, had what I term the rules of faith in common. In keeping the routines of their faith, they helped others and me gain success. What are these rules of faith?

One of my greatest teachers of ministry would say: "Luonne, plan the work and work the plan." You may ask, "How is that taking a walk of faith?" There is no "good plan" without God. Nothing in life is good without God. In fact, all of life would be good if humanity would not turn away from God. You may argue the point, but pray and discover the reality. Within planning and working we find the rules of faith:

1. Trust your thoughts to be guided by God.

2. Trust your desirable outcomes to the will of God.

3. Trust your abilities to carry out what God has purposed you to do.

4. Trust the implementation of plans born from your thoughts and informed by your research.

5. Trust your methods of passing on the insights granted by grace unto you.

6. Trust your working each step of the plan of implementation with feasible actions.

7. Trust the results of your process to God.

In so living by the rules of faith, the wisdom writer affirms success and prosperity. Marie is an example of this truth. She soars. Let the wise follow suit by taking no shortcut toward the destination. Too many students of shortcuts are cut short on successful living.

Prayer: "Lord Jesus Christ, Son of God, grant mercy and healing upon us, who grieve. Amen."

Day 35

FREEDOM

Read: Habakkuk 3

There is freedom in obedience to God. Key to freedom is full compliance to the will of God. Charles Stanley, renowned preacher in Atlanta, Georgia, states: "Partial obedience is no obedience at all, if we are to walk with God, we must listen to what He says--all of what He says." Moses in response to the call of God led the children Israel out of Egyptian bondage. The Word reveals that God heard their desire to serve the Lord, and delivered them.

A newspaper in the South records: "Selling Slavery." Business people in the area are marketing the history of American slavery. Being as I am, it struck a chord of discord within me. I know why. My ancestors were victims of the inhumane system of American slavery. There were years of not being paid for labor on plantations. Today, ancestors of plantation owners appear interested in profiting from "selling slavery" in the market places where slaves were held in bondage to be sold at auctions.

A few Blacks are on board with the projects. They are even getting some cash from the show. There are many ancestors of slaves, who are still waiting for cash from the historical reality of the profiting of Americans off the free labor of African slaves. The election of a Black male or female to the White House will be political progress, but changes little in freedom. Still it will not grant the economic freedom promised in "forty acres and a mule."

American freedom will never be freedom, until freedom is holistic. Partial freedom is not freedom at all, if we are to be free in America; we need to obey the Word of God, beyond the laws of the land. In the Word of God truth is to be found. A truth of justice and doing unto others as you would have them do unto you. True freedom would bring about reparations, so that America is guilt free and forgiven.

I am asking that we end the business of "selling slavery," and finish the business of "ending slavery." Peace without justice is no peace at all. Deliverance is not complete until America delivers on the promise of reparation. "Give us; Us fees!" Deliver the land and the means to cultivate it. Grief in wrong doing is as sorrow in death; it pains until resurrection day is matched with repenting hearts and minds.

Prayer: "Lord Jesus Christ, Son of God, grant mercy and healing upon us, who grieve. Amen."

Day 36

EXPERIENCE OF LIFE

Read: Zephaniah 3

I enjoy listening to music on a rainy day. On one day while jamming, a text message came through. It announced the accidental death of a young man, who I never met. Our connection was through his scouting with a member of my church, who was his friend. Dead at the age of 22 years…grief shocked people. His younger brother once spoke at our community of faith.

He experienced life.

Now he has the experience of death.

A beloved friend died in an automobile accident at the age of 65 years. While driving his car, someone illegally crossed the opposite median. When it happened, I had no questions. My experience of life had taught me that questions change nothing. I had to accept the hurt and pain of lost, then look for the gain of heaven and toward a life beyond death. I look to Jesus Christ as the source of eternal life.

I do not know much about our scout's friend. I know more about my friend and all I know about him was good. My knowledge or lack of knowledge doesn't change the experience of life. All of the knowing in the world will not prevent us from living or dying. There is only one source that changes our experience of life and death, who is God. God is the Source of Life. I choose to believe in God and have faith in Jesus Christ!

Could not Jesus, who performs miracles, have kept these men from dying? He did, not because of what we know about them beyond the fact of faith. He kept them from dying by accepting them into the arms of grace and mercy, which was granted at their entrance into life and confirmed in their acceptance of the reality that life is eternal. By faith are people of God made whole! By faith we worship and our works through the experience of life expose the reality of our eternity. By faith! I believe!

When I come to die, give me Jesus, then my experience of life knows not the end.

Prayer: "Lord Jesus Christ, Son of God, grant mercy and healing upon us, who grieve. Amen."

Day 37

BEYOND THE WALLS

Read: Haggai 2

I was very excited when the Lord spoke and my congregation returned to street evangelism. They offered people what has forever been available in the walls of the church, but too many people are beyond the walls never experiencing the riches of faith. People beyond the walls are not coming within our churches and we, too often, are not going beyond the walls.

The move from spiritual depravity into spiritual formation is as simple as believing in Jesus Christ, and as challenging as believing in Jesus Christ. Faith is the way of salvation and healing, if we believe, so it is taught in the Gospel of Mark 5th Chapter. However, believing in Jesus Christ is more than word of mouth. Believing in Jesus Christ is living by the Word of God as revealed in the Holy Scripture and experienced through the touch of the power of the Holy Spirit.

I was ecstatic when my people became energized and motivated to offer unto all that which can transform the life of anyone with ears to hear. What is the message coming forth to change lives and prayerfully bring in new converts?

1. Holy Communion is the blessed discipline of seeking peace with God.

2. Prayer is vowing to bow unto the will of God.

3. Preaching and witnessing beyond the walls of the church in making of disciples of Jesus Christ.

4. The method of evangelism is to bless the unblessed.

5. Winners pray not to win, they pray to be sustained in winning.

6. Share personal faith in Jesus Christ, so as to build a corporate body of Jesus Christ – the Church.

We should all go beyond the walls of our local churches and bring new converts within the walls of our churches. Bringing Jesus Christ beyond the walls is the only means of winning souls in the streets. There are people dying in the streets…Jesus is the answer to living unto eternal life.

Prayer: "Lord Jesus Christ, Son of God, grant mercy and healing upon us, who grieve. Amen."

Day 38

DARKNESS OF A HUMAN HEART

Read: Zechariah 14

In July of 2008, I preached a series on "Go to Hell Judas!"

I know there can only be one Judas, because there is only one Jesus.

We do not have another master of the "darkest human heart," in there is not another Master of our souls to save us.

What we have in the world today has to do with the Judas mindset over against those who with the heart of God seek to be like Jesus. In my heart, in my mind, in my loving, and my entire being - I want to be like Jesus.

What about those who are like minded to Judas? Imagine finding a friend, who would turn on you as Judas turned on Jesus. Sorry, I cannot even imagine a friend having such darkness of a human heart. Those of you who encountered such darkness early in life, it had to be horrible living so many years in suspect of friends turning on you or turning you in. "Cheesing, is what it was call in the days of my youth. Well, at the age of 50 I did not have to imagine it, I experienced being betrayed by a friend among friends and in the instant I suspect that everyone was a potential backstabbing betrayer. It is miserable living in suspect, because you soon begin to drown in the puke of such misery. Well, what do you do, when you have done your best and friends seem too far a distance away? I found the answer I had all the time. It is the answer dwelling with all believers… Jesus.

Then, I studied again the story of Jesus. Believing in Jesus humbles me to my worthless state of being void of Christ. Who am I to judge though judged, when I know my worth is due to Christ dying even for me. In so dying for me, He died for all believing in Him. I quickly let go of the feelings and suspicious behavior toward all. Not everyone has a Judas mindset. Even so, my prayer is for the poison in the heart of my so-call friend and others in the mindset of Judas to be removed.

May those whom we consider friends, who betray and back-bite be transformed within their hearts and come to live with the mind of Jesus Christ.

Judas should never be considered godly. Persons in the likeness of Judas are like dirty and diseased dogs. They are liars who smile in your face, while awaiting moments to destroy you with a traitor's kiss. Cunning and tricky! Yes, indeed, they are, but we must pray for them as Jesus prays even for the likes of Judas. They may be persons who sit beside you in church pews. They may be confessed so-called Christians, who are insincere and praying on your turf. The bible says, "Watch them dogs!" Watch them, indeed, however, in the end it is not about you or me. No, no, no! It is never really a sin against us. The sin is always against God. Just know that whomever they may be, their arms are certainly too short to box with God. Good always wins for God is the originator of good and all that is good and perfect comes from God...God and God alone.

A challenge for us each day is to examine ourselves and ask as we see ourselves in the mirrors of our souls, "What kiss am I leaving upon the cheeks of others? Is it sincere and holy or is it like the Judas' kiss?"

Prayer: "Lord Jesus Christ, Son of God, grant mercy and healing upon us, who grieve. Amen."

Day 39

REASONS FOR PRAYER

Read: Malachi 3

Jesus prayed for me. Why?

And, if you believe in him through the Word of his disciples, He prayed for you, too. Why?

The Gospel of John reveals that Jesus prayed for Himself, for His disciples, and for all believers. In John 17th Chapter of the revealing Word, Jesus is praying. I love that Jesus prayed for us. What touches me most is not that the Savior would pray for us, but the reasons for His praying.

1. He prayed for our unity - oneness. That we might come together in spiritual unity with God and our Savior. Believing that God sent Jesus for our salvation. Jesus prayed for us!

2. He prayed that we may know the love of God. To be loved by God, and know it. Jesus prayed for us!

3. He prayed that we may share in the glory of being children of God. Here and now on earth we are to be in the glory of God. Jesus prayed for us!

Let us cherish the love given to us by God. We have this love because we are worth it. We are worthy of being loved, in that we are good creations of God. With all that is within we know and we love the One who has given life to us.

Because God loves us, we want to follow the Word of God. We want to be like Jesus and abide in the Word as the Word abides in us. We want to share in the mission of Jesus Christ and soak in the glory of God. We are not ashamed of God. We are not ashamed to live in the Prince of peace or embodiment of the King of kings. We want to be like Jesus.

Prayer: "Lord Jesus Christ, Son of God, grant mercy and healing upon us, who grieve. Amen."

Day 40

STANDING FOR OR AGAINST JESUS

Read: Matthew 12

Three groups of persons are reflected in Matthew's Gospel as having the opportunity to stand for or against Jesus: Jesus' disciples; the crowds; and the Jewish leaders.

The disciples, with the exception of Judas Iscariot, stood with Jesus, especially post His resurrection. We also know that the Jewish leaders stood against Him, and ultimately turned a once admiring crowd into a people asking for the death of Jesus. Wow! How soon people can change.

Faith seldom views movies. However, LOVE led her into the theatre when asked to view Hancock. Hancock, a superhero, while helping the crowd was ripping the City of Angeles apart. The crowd disliked him. An image maker took interest in changing the image of his hero. He convinced Hancock to serve a term in prison for the havoc he had placed on the city, until the people called for him. Surely, when they needed him most, he came through outfitted to save good people and punish the bad guys. His image was given new birth, when he rescued the city from criminals. Wow! How soon people can change.

Some people never change soon enough. In fact, some may never change. In a manual on discipleship, "Matthew exalts Jesus as the supreme Lord and teacher of the historical disciples and the post resurrection community." (M.J. Wilkins) If the Gospel of Matthew can be the manual, then Jesus must be the model for discipleship. Jesus called, trained, and commissioned the disciples to carry out the great mandate to "make disciples." If Faith could be influenced to view a movie, most people may respond to the authority given believers to bring individuals to seeing Jesus. Wow! People can quickly change.

The plan of evangelism is real simple and plain - give people Jesus. Jesus' calls us to a life of obedience, accountability in discipleship groups, costly allegiance to the ministry, and fellowship with diversity of people. We are to follow Jesus faithfully attached, continuing to count the cost, becoming like Jesus preaching the same message, teaching the same ministry, and showing the same compassion. So that commissioned by Jesus, we make disciples throughout the communities, baptizing in the name of the Father, Son, and Holy Spirit. We are to teach people to be obedient, because know Jesus is with us always and forever.

Now is the time to hear the Savior calling and invite five people weekly to come follow Jesus, and be baptized in the Name. We will teach you, and faith will save you. Yes, we are people, and we can quickly change. Have you brought five people to Christ this year? Change now and bring in five times five: twenty-five church members. Wow! People can change, will you?

People die quickly, too. When death comes into your experience it changes the paradigm of existence. Someone is never to be in your human state of existence again. People die and so will you; so will I. The question for us has not to do with the when, how and why of death. The sensible question of faith has to do with our state of readiness. Will you be ready when our Savior comes? Are you ready for the glorification of God? Here and now, shall you give your life unto God, so as to live and never die? For the Word of God is truth: Whosoever believeth in Him, shall not perish, but have everlasting life. (John 3:16)

Judas stood against Jesus; I am standing for Jesus against all comers, now and forevermore.

Are you standing for or against Jesus?

Prayer: "Lord Jesus Christ, Son of God, grant mercy and healing upon us, who grieve. Amen."

Day 41

GO TO HELL JUDAS

Read: Mark 8

Did Judas go to heaven or hell?

I discovered most people asking the question of Judas' afterlife struggle with lives as lived by loved ones or with their own undesirable challenges. How are you to respond to persons concerned with the aftermath of living? We are going to die just as sure as we live. Do we just live, so as to eat and drink and be merry... shouting: "To hell with the rest of the world, I am going to have it my way, baby!"

Some have attempted to answer the question based on logic.

Others answer the heaven or hell question of Judas based on the nature of a forgiving God, who foreordained Judas to do what he had no choice, but to do as he did – betray Jesus.

Then, there are those who do not care where Judas is or where they are going, they just want to live and let live. What the hell is heaven or what in heaven is hell?

One thing for sure, Judas had every opportunity to change his mind. God has so designed the world that we have free will. Our free will does not change the ultimate of God's plan. However, it may alter how the plan is carried out.

God created the world for a right relationship with humankind. Human sin altered the means of the relationship. Still, the act of Jesus Christ as a means of grace brought back the ultimate of the will of God. Through Christ we are brought into right relationship with God. *"For God so loved the world that He gave His only Begotten Son, that whoever believes in him should not parish but have everlasting life."* (John 3:16 NKJV)

James Farmer, Sr. is reflected on in a movie as having asked his son: "Junior, what is the greatest weakness of man?" Junior answered: "Doubt; Disbelief." Failure to believe in Jesus as the true Christ/Messiah was the greatest weakness of Judas. Judas had, like every other human, many flaws but none greater than his doubt in Jesus as the Messiah. His doubt led him to turn Jesus over, not his sinful lust, greed, or even love for money. It was his lack of assurance that Jesus was actually who he claimed to be. So, when he was fed up with the leadership of the one he came to believe was the great pretender, Judas betrayed Jesus. It is not enough to confess Christ and join the church. We need to give Christ our hearts, and give our minds Christ. The love of Jesus Christ will bring us to open our hearts and let faith in Jesus abide. If we let Jesus in, we will come to know He is our Savior, Lord of lords, King of kings, the Son of God. Judas never came to believe. Jesus announced to God that he had kept all who the Father had given Him, except the one who God knew would be faking good until the day of betrayal.

Peter acknowledged that Judas having betrayed Jesus was lost and fell to his death with his internal parts bursting out of his body. Peter also *"said to them, 'Repent and let every one of you be baptized in the name of Jesus Christ for the remission of sins; and you shall receive the gift of the Holy Spirit.'"* (Acts 2:38 NKJV) Judas never came to believe in Jesus as Messiah, and failed to repent once he witnessed the sentencing of an innocent man, who he betrayed. Did Judas go to heaven or hell? You choose.

This has been written for the grief experiences of human beings from the holiness of sincerity of hearts to the darkness of hearts with mindsets of Judas. In the end, the way to move beyond the dreadful experience of grief is to move into the joyous experience of glorification. You may know your state of readiness to move on with or without grief by the way you answer one question: Will you go to heaven or hell?

It is not your choice. It is God's choice. Your choice is only whether or not to believe that Jesus is the Son of God, was crucified, dead and buried, born of a virgin, rose on the third day and sits at the right hand of God the Father where He has created a place for all who believe. I believe! If heaven was not promised to believers, I still would choose Jesus. Do you?

In essence, worry not for your soul or the souls of people, who, too, have come to know God. If you do not know God as the source of all that has been, all that is and all that shall be forevermore. I invite you now, to pray in the name of Jesus:

Prayer: "Lord Jesus Christ, Son of God, grant mercy and healing upon us, who grieve. Amen."

Day 42

AUTHENTIC LOVE OF GOD AND OTHERS

Read: Luke 15

There lived a woman whose death was an expected unexpected reality. Never dreamed she would die so soon. A most impressive woman! She was not my laptop theologian. She was though a "theologian of the practical." One of the philosophical expressions realized in her actions was doing acts of goodness "for the sake of goodness." In other words, she did things right, while seeking to do right things. With her faith grounded in Jesus Christ, she was one of the women who had no shame in appreciating the theology of the Apostle Paul. While she learned the teachings of Paul to Timothy, she lived as though directly taught by Jesus Christ. With sincerity of heart, she loved God and sought to love others as she desired to be loved by people. She was loved, yet no greater was the love shown to her than the love she gave to others. She shall be missed, for sure.

When she died, her grandchild stated: "Grandma loved you Dad! There are pictures of you in practically every room." On the surface it is easy to consider it was about him. But was it really about him or was it all about her love for Jesus Christ. She held great admiration for the call to discipleship on the life of her son-in-law. Her love for God was represented in him. In a real sense, their bond was in the leap of faith. He was not her lap child, yet their conversations about God were food for the soul. While drinking coffee in her home, he would listen to her joy in the Lord. They shared a mutual love of God and heart for the well-being of people. Though she died, yet does she live! And the pictures of a dear mother-in-law continue to abide on the walls of his heart.

Writings of Soren Kierkegaard "upholds the idea that every human being exists in one of three spheres (or on planes) of existence, the aesthetic, ethical, and religious. Most people, he observed, live an aesthetic life in which nothing matters but appearances, pleasures, and happiness. It is in accordance with the desires in this sphere that people follow social conventions. Kierkegaard also considered the violation of social conventions for personal reasons (e.g., in the pursuit of fame, reputation for rebelliousness) to be a personal aesthetic choice. A much smaller group consists of persons, who live in the ethical sphere trying their best to do the right thing. They see past the shallow pleasantries and ideas of society. The third and highest sphere is the faith sphere. To be in the faith sphere: How could Kierkegaard mean anymore than one must give the entirety of oneself to God? The challenge to becoming an "authentic being" on the plane of faith has to do with total surrender to God.

She lived as a practical example of a life in surrender to God. Persons witnessing to her life acknowledged that at her resurrection service. While listening to their witness to her life, I thought of my own. Have you ever done that at a memorial or funeral service? I did. I thought of times when I have, in the likeness of John Wesley, wondered if I have been truly authentic in my Christian faith. Am I Christian? Have I ever been? Since there is not an almost Christian, you are either Christian or you are not Christian. Am I a Christian?

Today assuredly, I am a child of God. I live into the purpose of my birth. I was born into the purpose for which I live. I live to love in the spirit of Agape-the highest form of godly love known to human beings. Like my practical theologian, who has crossed over into eternal life beyond death, I am taking the leap of faith. My life belongs to God, because I am a disciple of Jesus Christ by faith. Right or wrong, it's my choice and I am staying with it. I came to this not by "intelligent design," but by faith in my experience of Jesus as Christ. Yes, I am a Christian! Praise God!

Prayer: "Lord Jesus Christ, Son of God, grant mercy and healing upon us, who grieve. Amen."

Day 43

TIME OF TROUBLE

Read: John 3

Jesus was asleep, when the boat tossed and whirled on troubled waters was a source of fear for his disciples. According to Matthew, 8:23-27, he may have been exhausted from a great days work, yet still processed authority to calm the stormy sea. He was a traveling man, busy about the business of God. His confidence and faith in God was remarkable. He knew God would sustain Him through the storms of life. So, exhausted, but not withstanding filled with power he utter: "Peace, be still." (Mark 4:39 NKJV)

> Help me, O Lord, in Thy plan to believe;
> Help me, my fragment each day to receive;
> Oh that my will may with Thine have no strife!
> Since God-yielded wills find the God-planned life.
> -Author Unknown

Averaging four hours of sleep daily, sometime I just want to sleep soundly. Some nights working without moments of closed eyes; Why? Choosing to work or sleep, peace of mind is in knowing that in all things and through all times there is the comfort of God. Existence in every form is dependent upon God. God sustains life, which at times has men and women struggle to find all good in God when all is not good in the world. So, waking or sleeping, my hope and trust is in the divine design of our Creator. I surrender thoughts and feelings into the Essential Existence that is beyond full comprehension, yet understood. I love God!

Never alone are we in life. In fact, sleeping four hours, more or less, is not meant to be idly drifting meaningless in the world. In sleep we are providing supportive ways and means of sustaining life within bodies granted us, so as to be able to support life in our waking hours of life granted humanity. We are not alone. We are here to assist, rather near or far, others. We are to live in a supportive humanity, which includes life's existence throughout the world. .

Prayer: "Lord Jesus Christ, Son of God, grant mercy and healing upon us, who grieve. Amen."

Day 44

RELAXING WITH GOD

Read: Acts 2

Relaxing with God is different from bed rest. Sleeping is certainly not the same as spending "alert time" with God. Relaxing with God is the act of bringing your whole being to the attention of the Divine. Relaxing with God centers the mind and heart on spiritual realities. Our minds, too often, busy with matters in the world are carving relaxation. In the state of relaxation, listen for God.

There is real relaxing with God, when our minds are settled in a place of holiness. Within churches throughout the United States of America worshippers may sing: "*Come let us worship the Lord in the beauty of holiness.*" Have you been too busy to come? Come now from where you are to a mental place of worship. Set your mind at ease.

What is worshipping and living in the beauty of holiness? Holiness is living in communion with the Spirit of God, after being converted to faith in God. Acceptance of salvation is acknowledgement of grace given to the believer, knowing that you are such a believer. Sin no longer has influence over the faith of the forgiven. God removes sin's guilty stain. In order to live into holiness, believers step from the conversion experience into daily living in making the choice to "go and sin no more".

The beauty of holiness is living the transformed life. The way we used to live, we live no more. We die to sin and live the righteous life. Christ-likeness is seen in disciples of Jesus Christ. Christian worship is praising God in forgiveness of the confessing of sins and praying for the strength necessary to elevate sin in daily living. Praise for the goodness that is found beyond the acts unfounded in evil hearts. Praise worship lifts the victorious belief in overcoming hatred and bitterness. The beauty of holiness in worship has to do with baring fruit of love, joy, and peace, which yields kindness, goodness, patience, faithfulness, gentleness, and self-control even when faced with the most difficult people. Our victory is in living into the promises of God. God has promised unto all believers the opportunity to walk into the newness of life despite the presence of hate filled persons around us. Are you saved? Are you assured of being delivered from the enemies of life? If you have not yielded your life to Christ, do it now. Then, stand before all men and women, not only forgiven but with a heart to forgive.

Prayer: "Lord Jesus Christ, Son of God, grant mercy and healing upon us, who grieve. Amen." 🖊

Day 45

MOTHERS

Read: Romans 6-8

Good mothers are not always married. Some good mothers are single or widowed or divorced or living with significant others. In modern terminology, living with or without the "baby's daddy," blessed be the mothers, who love their children with tenderness, patience and control. Marriage is not a requirement for motherhood in civil laws of the United States of America. And, in the sacred communities a good and virtuous woman has the making of a good mother with or without a ring on it (a finger) or papers (legalize marriage certificates. When it's Mother's Day, who cares?

Since Mother's death in 2002, on Mother's Day, I wear the color white on the outside and on the inside I wear red. Red is the symbolic color for true love - the fruit of the spirit. There is a spirit of Mother's love that did not leave with her last breath. It is the spirit that refused to be buried in her grave. It is the spirit of love that she planted within me from June 22, 1955 unto April 15, 2002 and this spirit of love shall forever be in me.

The Samaritan Woman did not visit the office of Jesus in tears; did she? She had told him stories of giving a child away, when drugging and taking sexual liberties. Clean and living a life with no thought of "an unknown child," the woman at the well did not expect to be called out on a different form of motherhood and spousal responsibilities. It is called servant-hood in response to Jesus. The Samaritan woman at the well learned through the agape response of Jesus that physical, moral, cultural, sexual, etc... do not hinder the nurturing love of God. An encounter of divine love brought a woman to request more thirst quenching love, which Jesus offers forgiveness. The once unknown child of God was made known to her and she learned that as with loving mothers, the love of God, too, is unconditional. (John 4:1-26).

The only begotten child of God is the Savior – Jesus. His love is here for women and men with unknown children in the world. His love is here for daughter and son of the unknown biological parents. It is a caregiver's love offering to people accepting of the truth as well as the persons crying out from guilt of the known - unknown child.

Good Mothers, though they die, still live in the hearts of their children. For the Almighty designed it to be so. In so keeping, I pose the question: What color rose are you wearing on Mother's Day? And another is this: What color flower will your child wear on their heart while you are yet alive? Deeper still: For who is the flower worn; mother or unknown mother? Deeper still: What is the color of the flowers worn for God from whom flows the ultimate parental love?

Prayer: "Lord Jesus Christ, Son of God, grant mercy and healing upon us, who grieve. Amen."

Day 46

THE ENDING OF LIFE

Read: First Corinthians 13

Mother died on April 15, 2002. The experience of her loss was beyond anything ever felt. She is my Mother. It was different having her die. Different from witnessing the ending of life of another person, I saw my mother dead. She was the first female known to me. She taught me the stories of Jesus as I sat on her lap. She was my friend, teacher and true *Laptop Theologian*. And, in the end, she was still teaching me. Ten months later on February 19, 2003, my father died. Experiencing the death of Mother had taught me to accept the death and dying of my Father.

Death is the ending of life as we know it on earth. Accepting the reality of death and dying sent me to the Scriptures with human questions of God. "Why? Why now? Why MY parents? Why; why?" Thoughts of eternal life quickly came, and quickly lost influence on my weakened human emotions. My mind held the words of faith and my soul grasped the promised assurance of God's deliverance, but my heart ached and my eyes poured tears. I did not want to hear about faith or hope in eternity. I knew it all. I had heard it before. All of my life, Mother taught it and Daddy preached it. I needed not another sermon; I needed and wanted my parents.

My Mother and Father had died. Period! I would never see them again. And, then, I asked myself: "What do I do now?" My parents, who had met my needs and wants in life at the ending of life, could not meet my heart's strongest desire - eternal life now. They lived as long as they could but did not make their lives my eternity, because they knew Jesus Christ.

Jesus Christ paid the price for our glorious eternity. The Church at its best seeks to meet the needs of people not as objects of service, rather as children of God. Why? Because the Church is the body of Christ - Easter people - created for the care of humanity and faith in eternity. As Easter people, we celebrate the atoning act of God in Jesus of Nazareth. The doctrine of the atonement expresses the belief in the work of Christ as the act of reconciling God with humanity.

The ending of life is the beginning of life and dying in Christ makes it right. Oh, my parents bought eternity, when they taught me faith is Jesus Christ.

Prayer: "Lord Jesus Christ, Son of God, grant mercy and healing upon us, who grieve. Amen."

Day 47

BODY BUILDERS IN HOLY OBEDIENCE

Read: Second Corinthians 8 & 9

Body building for Christ has to do with living in holy obedience. During the observance of a holy Lent, participate in sharing 46 days on one accord praying and studying the Word of God (Bible). You may utilize a devotional guide. No one has to monitor your obedience. No one should force you to observe or even pick up a devotional or Bible. Every participant is at liberty to follow the leading of the Holy Spirit and build trust toward God. Beyond the norm of fasting, studying Scripture and praying without ceasing, it shall be a journey of hope. The hope of pastors remains deeply grounded within the faith that congregations will love with the Agape of God people throughout existence.

Disciples of Jesus are asked to spread sacrificial love through financial gifts beyond tithing of time, space, energy, and finance, in order to build the body of Christ in ministries with people. This spiritual journey to the cross is a walk in the light of love, annually knowing that the experience of the crucifixion is the ultimate realization of sacrifice for humanity. Love on the cross shown in the death and dying of Jesus. A love for the enemies of God, sinners against God and saints believing the love of God saves. The call is to be body builders in holy obedience, so as to have the kingdom of God on earth as The Church – The Body of Christ. The ideal community of faith unspoiled by sin, death, pain and sorrow is the desirable outcome of living in holy obedience. The Body of Christ is where people are to come seeking the face of God on the people of God and find God, who they seek. How can we do it? Good question!

Such love requires in most cases a new attitude. By faith people may renew minds, hearts, and souls as to believe in God, while showing respect, care and empathy in mutual listening and responding with persons in the community of faith. It is an intentionality of love. It is being alert to treating persons as we want to be treated as they are and unnecessary to how they treat us. Being in holy obedience is following the commandments of our covenant with God. Jesus taught that the covenant can be upheld by loving God with our whole being and our neighbors as ourselves.

Prayer: "Lord Jesus Christ, Son of God, grant mercy and healing upon us, who grieve. Amen."

Day 48

TIME TO VOTE; TIME TO CHANGE

Read: Galatians 4

Lord, is there a price I have to pay to live this way? The Christian life moving from the 20th century into the 21st century has been a challenge. Perhaps it has always been a challenge. Martin Luther King, Jr. wrote of the Christian life: *"Every true Christian is a citizen of two worlds, the world of time and the world of eternity."*

With a faith and hope of eternal bliss, Christians live amidst the currencies of existence. A declared election year in the United States of America denotes a need for prayer. Christian morality may not be a consideration in this process though the dollar declares, "In God we trust." In such time of history, however, every Christian should take a serious look at justice and fairness when casting a vote.

For the first time in history, we witnessed the election of an African American president, when President Barack H. Obama was elected. In writing these notes, there is an awareness that a female is out in front of candidates for the office of President in 2016. So, there may be a female elected president for the first time in the USA. The world is changing. Christians participating in elections through the centuries have in majority been conformists. Now it is time to hear a call to nonconformity. The challenge now is to live out of conviction, not conformity. The noble moral action would be to vote for the best candidate, regardless to the color of his or her skin or gender.

The law of the land dares a minister to cross certain lines in endorsing candidates for political office. The law of the land, therefore, may have clergy supporting conformity by being silent. Daring to respond to a higher order than the law of the land, I claim more than a social responsibility because I respond to the Moral Authority - God. I dare to encourage people of faith with moral integrity to vote for the most qualified candidate, even if that candidate is a woman. Is it personal? Yes, it is personal and an issue of social justice. It is personal, because I was born of woman's womb. It is personal, because I was born a Negro in the United States of America. It is personal, because I have witnessed the abuse of women and people of color in American politics from the 1950s into the 21st century. It is personal, because I want to see a just act among United States citizens in electing a person President without basing such election on ethnicity or gender. I want women and men of all races to have an equal opportunity to serve. I want them to have actual occupancy of the office of President and access to the White House as home.

I am a Christian with faith and hope in eternity. My time to love is here and now. Thus, in kindness with selfless love, I urge citizens of the United States in these times to cast a vote for justice and equality for men and women to be judged as Dr. King urged, "By the content of his or her character and not by the color of their skin." May God bless us all and may God bless America, land that we all love! And may those, who grief the past with it unjust ways of segregation and discrimination find peace in these words: I understand the grief of not having your own way, so I offer you the strength and wisdom that sustained me and others through these gruesome years – God. "Trust in the Lord with all of your heart, and lean not on your own understanding. In all of your ways acknowledge Him and He shall direct your path." (Proverbs 3:5-6 NKJV)

Prayer: "Lord Jesus Christ, Son of God, grant mercy and healing upon us, who grieve. Amen."

Day 49

Epiphany to Lent

Read Ephesians 6

On Ash Wednesday things will change.

The light of the world will become the sufferer of life. It seems too soon.

On the first day of January, annually Christians and others may celebrate the birth of Mary's baby - Jesus.

Now look and listen as songs have turned from praise of birth to hymns and music for a season of ministry, before death. What makes it bad or sad? Why is it that often a madding sense of frustration comes, after such a celebration of life? Well, listen to the answer in the music.

Epiphany sounds in "We Three Kings", "Joy to The World" and "Silent Night" sung in praise for the light of the world and the manifestation of the Anointed One. Now, moving from Epiphany into Lent, songs bring a paradigm shift from praise singing to songs of the cross, such as "The Old Rugged Cross."

The Old Rugged Cross is a favorite hymn. It should never be demeaned. Oh no! In fact sing it as though the cross is personal, for it is. It is on the cross that human life is restored. On the cross is where salvation of the soul is to be found. On the cross Jesus died for you and me. Oh, yes, "I love that old cross."

Yet, it is in the movement from singing celebration birth songs that we move to resurrection from death songs and are made to wonder.

Wonder how it is that God would love humanity so as to give his only Son for all souls. How could it be?

Love! At the birth of Mary's baby the gifts for life came to Him; at the death of Jesus Christ gift of life is given the world for all generations over. God so loved the world that he gave Jesus, The Anointed One, as savior for all who come to believe. Do you believe?

Believe the gift of life is eternal through the acts of God. If you believe, then join Christians on Ash Wednesday and journey for 46 days of spiritual growth. Bathe in the experience of the gift of life. The gift of life was bought by God and granted the world at the cost of his Beloved Son - Jesus!

Come as you are praying and studying, so as to accept what God has done through Christ. Then, leave the experience of being you to living the experience of God in you. People change. Everything can change. The change could happen on Ash Wednesday or on Thursday. In fact, the magic is not in the day of the week or hour. The blessing is in taking the leap of faith on the adventurous journey to the Cross. The promised change will come. Try it!

Read daily Scripture, which lead from the temptation of Jesus in the wilderness post the Baptism of our Lord to His triumphant entry into Jerusalem on Palm Sunday. Then, journey through the Holy Week experience onto the day of Resurrection. Easter! When Jesus Christ arises and gives life a new song. Change! Great change from Epiphany to Lent. Even greater may be the change into Easter.

Come, Lord Jesus, change us.

Prayer: "Lord Jesus Christ, Son of God, grant mercy and healing upon us, who grieve. Amen."

Day 50

WHERE IS JESUS?

Read: Philippians 2

Epiphany is the day of our Lord's manifestation. It was originally celebrated by Christians even more than Christmas Day. The celebration of the Epiphany recognizes the nativity, incarnation and baptism of Christ. Recalling of the visit of the three wise men (magi), which marks the end of the Christmas cycle, it is a time of exchanging the gift of life for the Gift of Life. The King of kings is given the world by divine selection not human election. King Herod desired to kill him. Some people ignored him. Wise men come to see him.

Bringing gifts signifying the Lordship of the Jesus as the Christ child for the world was a tradition that I learned as a child in church. I recall the lesson taught in Centenary Methodist Episcopal Church from 1960 to 1964, when it first registered within my mind that Jesus, Mary's baby, is the King of the kingdom of God on earth. As a child, I came to believe the teachings and desired to tell the world. My father said: "Wait."

Christmases playing with the toys, riding new bikes and placing other treasures in storage would annually come and go. Constant would be our times of prayer and worship centering on Jesus as the Son of God. Mother would tell her sons to hurry, if we wanted to ride with her to church or we could walk the quarter of a mile from the parsonage on Sixth Street in Hartsville to Centenary MEC. Often she would leave saying: "Alright boys, I am going. Stick like glue bringing your brother on time", she spoke to my brothers urging them to hold my hand crossing the one street in the small town. I would hesitate in getting dress, so my brothers, not wanting to be frowned upon for being late, would finally say: "Come on, Luonne, you are going just as you are." Then, I would rush into my clothes to keep from being ashamed dressed in shorts.

Walking to the church, we could hear the singing almost a block away as the windows were often opened. "Come to Jesus" was a favorite back in the day. "Come to Jesus, right now. Right now; right now. Come to Jesus, right now." Wow ... I can still hear him at the end of the singing, Dad would say in preacher tone: "Come with your joys. Come have your thirst for life quenched. Come that your aches may be healed. Come to Jesus, the King of kings is waiting for you to follow his star, so come. Come as you are." As a child I would wonder: Where are you, Jesus? Then, they would have a recent born child or a baby doll in a crib, so as to make the story of the birth of Jesus live before our eyes. I believed!

Jesus is no longer in the nativity scene. He is not wrapped in swaddling clothes. He is not lying next to the animals in the wooden manger. There are no shepherds watching their flock by night. No star shines in the sky over the place in Bethlehem where the baby was laid. The questions have been asked and answered and the first plot thwarted. No, you will not find him on the lap of Mother Mary or nestled in her arms. Where is Jesus?

Jesus is in the heart, soul, and mind of all who believe that he is Christ, the Anointed Son of God. Do you believe?

I still believe. Now then, I invite you to "come, let us worship the Lord in the beauty of holiness". Come as you are even in shorts, there is no shame in being as you. Come as you are and be transformed into the garments God have prepared for you. Come to Jesus, right now. Jesus will save, He will heal you and He will give you the blessed assurance of eternal life, right now. After all, Christmas is really about the epiphany of Emmanuel – God is with us through life and death – we are eternal in God.

Prayer: "Lord Jesus Christ, Son of God, grant mercy and healing upon us, who grieve. Amen."

Day 51

BITTER SWEET BLESSINGS

Read: Colossians 3

Practice of psychotherapy has bitter sweet blessings. Skilled care is necessitated by revelation from clients. Molestation, rape, infidelity and issues from crisis are brought to individual or group session by persons seeking recovery through expert assistance. Persons often come to pastoral psychotherapists with the goal of quick fixes, then discover that life provides bitter and sweet experiences, which require for them instant gratification.

The story of Marah and Elim reveals Moses leading the people of Israel from the Red Sea crossing into the Desert of Shur. Three days into the journey water was yet to be found. When they arrived at Marah, the water there was too bitter to drink. The people grumbled against their leader and asked: "What are we to drink." Moses cried unto the Lord, and the Lord led him to wood, which was thrown into the water and the water became sweet. Then the Lord tested them saying: "If you listen carefully to the voice of the Lord, your God, and do what is right in His eyes, if you pay attention to His commands and keep all His decrees, I will not bring on you any of the diseases I brought on the Egyptians, for I am the Lord, who heals you." Perhaps for the moment they passed the test and came to Elim, where there were twelve springs and seventy palm trees around which they camped. They were blessed with assurance of more than enough. Psychotherapy by any means leads individuals through the tests of life, so as to know that individuals are provided more than enough to be sustained through the experiences of life.

The destruction in Haiti was not a test from God. I do not buy that theory or thought. What happened in Haiti on January 12, 2010 is a reality check on the damage an earthquake can bring. Apparently given no signs the crust of the earth erupted by way of its plates. People were wounded and some even killed as health

REV. DR. LUONNE ABRAM ROUSE

professionals from various places came to assist in a long term care process toward healing. A medical doctor was there, having departed a few days before the storm, she returned after the traumatic earthquake within a month and discovered an: "Oh my God" reality of life. The doctor went from the bitterness of sensitivity of human lost into the sweet experience of prayer for health. That is mental alertness and comprehension at its best, when the reality of mental shock amidst the traumas of life brings one to face the availability and possibility of healing, while holding you responsible and accountable for your actions and reactions in the course of experiences.

Bitter are the stories of pain and suffering, but "tis so sweet to trust God", who suffered Jesus for the salvation of the world. Believing in the gift of Jesus Christ, we face the experiences of life with a responsible nature seeking to be available to assist people in surviving the crises and storms.

Prayer: "Lord Jesus Christ, Son of God, grant mercy and healing upon us, who grieve. Amen."

Day 52

DIVINE FAMILY OF FAITH

Read: First Thessalonians 4

Islam is not the enemy of Christians. Christianity is not the enemy of Muslims. Christians and Muslims religions have never been enemies. People look in the mirror and pray the enemy away. Who or what is the enemy? The enemy is opposition to the will of God.

The nature of God for believers is goodness and righteousness. Followers of God cannot be soft on the doing of the will of God. In the Holy Scriptures of Jews and Christians, there is a teaching describing the duty of believers, which is also relevant to Muslims. Ecclesiastes 12:13 reads: "The end of the matter; all has been heard. Fear God, and keep his commandments; for that is the whole duty of everyone." (NRSV)

Religious leaders opposing the above may be suffering from the "spirit of the enemy". The spirit of the enemy will enlarge the ego of human beings, so as to have them yearning for fame and recognition. If for some reason they are denied their wishes, then they reflect a nature of passive-aggressiveness. After having presented themselves in the soft manner taught in the love nature of their faith, shame and pain in being disappointed even in small matters causes them to war against the so-called opposition. What should be done, when it seems that our views are not acceptable to humanity?

People of Islam and Christianity should take the "leap of faith", when it appears they are in bondage to the spirit of the enemy. Blind to the reality of being in opposition to the will of God, persons entangled by the ways of the enemy point fingers at others as being the reason for the discord. They refuse to accept that the current disappointment resulted from their living or speaking in opposition to God's will. What is the will of God?

Islam and Christianity are marked by love as the will of God. When love is lived among Muslims and Christians, then divine is the family of faith. The agape of God has diverse ways and means of being expressed. However, current scholarship has an understanding that the compassion required of Christians and Muslims is a challenge to live the faith proclaimed. Being born anew through prayer, repentance, surrender, and contentment, people of faith in both of these religions would benefit to seek unity in the midst of diversity. People of all religions are to turn to God for an understanding of ecumenism. Ecumenism has to do with the ability to lay down your differences and love the children of God from all walks of life. Ecumenism is the laying down of bitterness and praying for peace with justice, while maintaining righteousness.

We need healing through the power of prayer in all the land. Theology being the study of God in relation to humanity should be a blessed acceptance school of thought. It has to do with the thought of brothers and sisters born into the world not made by human being but created relatives by way of the Divine Allah - God. Shall our lives bear witness to the amazing grace of Our God, Our Creator? You choose; we are chosen to be the divine family of faith.

Prayer: "Lord Jesus Christ, Son of God, grant mercy and healing upon us, who grieve. Amen."

Day 53

FOREVERMORE

Read: Second Thessalonians 2

She changed her last name. Difficulties would find her much too soon in a divorce from the one person, who she loved enough to accept a name change. Whatever transpired, she handled life by making good decisions through it all. In one of the most significant cities in the United States of America, she came through public schools earning a university degree. She raised her children to be positive contributors in the world. She is a mother forever and a sister forever. She is really impressive. Amazing! The forevermore mark of exceptional character is her strength of endurance. She has relatives and friends, who are there through the sufferings and struggles. Have you ever been led to think what sisters do to survive the aloneness or the loneliness, when the presence seems lost in the wilderness?

A time for healing and reconciliation prayers; time for a yearning philosopher to feast on how precious love is beyond the self as brought to understanding by Soren Kierkegaard, the "singular universal" mark of universal significance that is known in his prolific writings on the matter of "ideal creatures" - women.

Reflecting back through the years, there among the assurances is the fact that a woman is a sister forevermore and in praying for her recovery, pray, too, how boys becoming men take girls to be precious women and then ... What follows the then in life? You choose.

Prayer: "Lord Jesus Christ, Son of God, grant mercy and healing upon us, who grieve. Amen."

Day 54

IRREPLACEABLE

Read: First Timothy 3

I was born into a parsonage family. From the moment of the merger of the Evangelical United Brethren Church with the Methodist Episcopal Church to form the United Methodist Church, I knew that I would devote my life to ordain ministry in the United Methodist Church. Without doubt, I am who I am in the United Methodist Church. Since 1975, laypeople have been irreplaceable in local churches I have served. The mere existence of a layperson in the pew means there is no other like that particular person. Existence proclaims a lay person to be irreplaceable...not prayers, not presence, not gifts, not service and not witness... mere existence speaks to the irreplaceable. This is no new thought it is seen from the beginning. Jesus is considered a second Adam, because the first Adam is still Adam and as irreplaceable as Eve.

Irreplaceable Friend! "IF" died 24 twenty years ago. Her existence in my life came suddenly and instantly as though we existed as sister and brother throughout life. Our families became family. Our days, weeks, months, and years were shared. Our children bonded. Our spouses called the other the moment one of us needed support. As sister and brother ought to be, we were friends. My friend is buried. During a gravesite visit, I stated: "Irreplaceable Friend", every year in observing All Saints Day, I will remember that you are 'IRREPLACEABLE". You see, love was not buried in the grave, because it is planted in the living heart.

May you, too, remember, no matter what... WE ARE IRREPLACEABLE!

Questions:

1. Several professional studies and personal experiences indicate that grief may be negative or positive. Particularly in the loss of spouses, significant others and children…human beings face the reality that many persons are experiencing deep sorrow growing as they face increasing pressure to survive while encountering many extra-unexpected activities resulting from death of loved ones. In turn, this causes these persons to place less emphasis on personal care. What has been your history of grief?

2. A church is a place of peace. The building is not the church – people are the Church. What has been your experience of the Church in response to grief?

3. Many churches have organized and trained pastoral care, but the bereavement ministries are not being utilized to measurable benefits. One way to examine this is the evaluation per active member. What is your evaluation of the current pastoral care in your local church?

4. Many congregations struggle with bereavement related issues – funeral costs, grief recovery, safety, pastoral accessibility, and even cosmetic attractiveness of deceased. How important is closure in the grief recovery process?

Prayer: "Lord Jesus Christ, Son of God, grant mercy and healing upon us, who grieve. Amen."

Day 55

INSPIRATIONS ARE DIVINE

Read: Second Timothy 2

President Barack Obama may have given inspiration to the world. Perhaps he placed the might of his office into the space program. A call for the necessary ways and means to control the space world is on point. President Obama may be the leader for the moment and future moments beyond his time. The decisions being made under his administration have the potential of bringing into fruition a merger of exploration and education for the extension of human understanding of the universe.

The earth serves a purpose of fulfillment for human existence as we understand it. The inspirations we have received from the Holy Scripture, which includes Jewish history and the relatedness of Gentiles to the same, are divine. Things are changing on earth, which threatens the good and safe existence of life on earth. It is a divine inspiration for leadership of the earth to think and plan beyond current existence into future possibility of life in the world beyond our known realities. Booster lifts in the process of reaching Mars with the possibility of life there and beyond is encouraging.

Though many of us may never see the full development of life on Mars or anywhere beyond the earth, we are witnessing the brilliance of the new frontier. More than exciting, it is inspiring. We have only the fear of God, when we have the means of securing life beyond the circumstance and changes in the environment as we have experienced it. There will be doubters, for sure. There will be skeptics, I know. Even I cannot believe, I lived to see it. Whatever your thoughts, remember this: Who born in 1955 thought that in 2007 that we would see a person of color elected President in the United States of America take the oath to lead our nation?

Then, it happened... In response to the Charleston Massacre, which occurred on June 17, 2015, President Obama delivered the eulogy for the nine persons murdered in Mother Emanuel African Methodist Episcopal Church, Charleston, SC. A South Carolina State Senator was among the nine persons murdered, so the President stepped up and eulogized, including the singing of "Amazing Grace." Death and dying may not only bring faith communities to a pause; indeed people nation-wide and world-wide are found in vital moments needing and desiring comfort and peace. In perhaps one of his greatest moments of leadership, President Obama served to people of the United States of America, practical care.

President Obama is running our nation as a visionary transforming the world. Join in saying: "Mr. President, we may not understand it all, but you are the elected President chosen to inspire us and change the course of history."

Prayer: "Lord Jesus Christ, Son of God, grant mercy and healing upon us, who grieve. Amen." ✐

Day 56

CALM AND QUIET

Read: Titus 2

On March 16, 2010, Geneva Blount Rouse told her beloved - she was tired. Within a few days "Granny Rouse" opened her eyes, took her last breath, closed her eyes and flew away.

A loving woman born in Robeson County, North Carolina with eight siblings, Granny Rouse was best known for loving her children. Most of her children preceded her in death. It was more of a blessing for them than for her heart, but that is another story. The story of her home going features the last of living children and her husband.

Granny moved in with them six years before she died. It was the blessing of a lifetime for our grandmother. Really! Superstars in care giving may be the best description of my aunt and uncle, who gave the best of love to their mother. When it came to the care of Granny Rouse, they did it right!

Granny Rouse had a terrible fall, which she never fully recovered from. Our aunt and uncle never failed in caring for her, providing angelic care that included precious home attendants. Applause! She was so excited about being with them. She never mentioned it to me, but I knew there was no way she was going to do the nursing home or assisted living business. It is good for some, for sure, but there was nothing better than being at home and maintaining a dignity of life for Granny Rouse. So, before her health went completely down, she was safe at home with family and home attendants, who became as family.

Over thirty four years in ministry, including clinical training as a therapist, I grieve in the "calm and quiet." I was encouraged by Granny Rouse to master the art of calm and quiet grief processing. She once told me at the death of my parents: "If you are crying now, Boy, you will not be able to do my funeral." There was always a known sense of my deep love between us, perhaps matching her deep love for people in general, but it felt extra special. Everyone, who came to know Geneva Rouse, could feel comfortable and loved. My Mother had a chorus of asking from time to time: "Does Granny Rouse know that I am your Mother, she thinks you love her more than me." I use to chuckle, because she also said with mutual love: "Granny Rouse is my best friend."

Granny Rouse had a way of bringing you into her best, and allowing your best to be given to her. Because of her best ways and means, the best of my grief processing has come in the form of what I call a "level headed ministry." A level head is necessary to comprehend the full experience of a life lived. In the midst of the calm and quiet Auntie G informed me: "Well, she is gone". I heard an immediate inner voice saying - "wipe your tears and live."

I desire Auntie G and Uncle G to wipe their tears and live. They gave so much of themselves through the years. Now it changes. The voice asking for fish and other items of a delicious meal will no longer be heard. Change comes, but not always easy.

When care givers transition into bereavement, persons who love them may offer 1000 ways to help wipe the tears and provide loving opportunities for life to be lived to the full extent.

Wow! Granny Rouse lived over 98 years, and still lives on. She is abiding now with our God, who dries weeping eyes and grants eternal life. To all who are lachrymose there is one command: "dry your eyes and live." Auntie G and Uncle G, we love you!

Prayer: "Lord Jesus Christ, Son of God, grant mercy and healing upon us, who grieve. Amen."

Day 57

GIVING THANKS FOR THE LUDICROUS

Read: Philemon 16, 17

"Those who find their life will lose it, and those who lose their life for my sake will find it." (Matthew 10:39) JB appeared at our local church on the night of his 29th birthday. He said that he lost his life and needed to be restored. In the process of being restored, he had no place to live, not even a shelter would be possible for him. On that night, he felt he had no place to lay his head beyond the church, which has "open hearts, open minds, and open doors."

The vision of the local church is clearly stated on the back of Sunday morning bulletins: "... is a body of Christ responding to the challenging call to love with compassion the children of God. Through Christ centered worship, we strive to achieve spiritual growth, and development with congregational outreach ministries that address the personal, social, and spiritual needs of the interfaith community."

Members are challenged to show respect, care, clear listening, and empathy with a young man they have never heard or met before. As uncomfortable as it is, this congregation of Christians may be called to be courageous in the outreach ministries toward the homeless. The required information by background check may not be given. The senior pastor has to decide even to ask or not ask for a background check. Odd, you say? In error, you pronounce? Understand, the homeless have been welcomed by a few beyond the senior pastor. His identity is not known among the elite. So, it may be miraculous for the church to permit housing a homeless person in the church facilities.

The evidence of identity for a homeless man, seeking help was now found as the professional rapper he claimed to be. Among other homeless in the area he was not known, because he has been inside the local church and not on the outside with the marginalized. The miracle that happened was truly by the grace of God because he is yet to be identified, while those who supported the senior pastor to allow the man off the street into the church during working hours were, too, called ludicrous.

Who he is really, may never be known? Over the days he spent in the church he became known as "the ludicrous" the church became thankful to have around. In thanksgiving for the grace of God a "so-called ludicrous" belief would proclaim an unknown homeless man is, too, a child of God needing the miraculous act of agape. The miraculous god given love to the homeless man may have been the best security personnel in the life of the church. He died and I still am giving thanks for the ludicrous belief that protected me on the streets and in the church. I officiated at his service … with thanksgiving.

Prayer: "Lord Jesus Christ, Son of God, grant mercy and healing upon us, who grieve. Amen."

Day 58

CIVIL RIGHTS MOVEMENT:
HISTORICAL & THEOLOGICAL PERSPECTIVE

Read: Hebrews 11

When African Americans were known as Negroes in the United States of America, they rose in the mid 1950's to form a "new" Civil Rights Movement in the nation. Throughout the USA, people of color were waiting for the National Association for the Advancement of Colored of People (NAACP) to achieve goals of freedom with justice for all in the land. The progress was too slow for the people in the south, who were being denied respectable seating on the bus, when whites came aboard. Eating establishments and other public facilities, including schools were segregated. Discrimination made separate, but equal a first class joke and a dream deferred.

While many had prepared themselves to make success in the battle of life, the cause for liberation needed a leader. One man was chosen in Montgomery, Alabama to head a movement protesting discrimination in public transportation. Historically known as the Montgomery Boycott, the young preacher recently graduated from Boston with a PhD. in Sacred Theology, Martin Luther King, Jr. was chosen as the voice of the people. He came to be more than a voice. Martin adhered to the call of God and became the sacrificial lamb. Mercy!

During the months of January (he was born on the 15th day of the first month of the year in 1928) and February (known for Black History Month), many people view the contributions of MLK, Jr. and other important leaders in the civil rights movement. Yet, when we pass through March, we enter the reality of April 4, 1968, when Dr. King was rifled down and his mind blown into death with the cessation of his life. Mercy!

On that 4th day of April in 1968, pause became the reality for the civil rights movement. In many ways, we have been pausing ever since. There has been no comparison leadership equal to the prolific oratory and wisdom of Martin Luther King, Jr. What has happen among the people now called African Americans is a moment by moment mentality of acceptance and toleration that too often resembles a need for recycling. In a time that is calling for repentance, in order to achieve reconciliation, people are pausing to celebrate a few social advances, slow political progress, and joyous entertainment economics. What has been good for the so-called gifted and talented, has left the United States of America drenched in sorrows and sufferings of the poor of every race, creed and color of people. Along with the African American, who is ever so reminded that to be Black is different and not always acceptable, people of every ethnicity is feeling the need for change.

Martin Luther King, Jr. stated on the last night of his living something resembling a Mosiac experience: "I have been to the mountaintop, and I have seen the Promised Land. I may not get there with you. But I want you to know tonight that we as a people will get to the Promised Land." The Promised Land, Canaan, the so-called heaven on earth was seen but not entered by Moses. Moses was not allowed to enter "because" he had broken "faith with" God "in the presence of the Israelites at the waters of Meribah Kadesh in the Desert of Zin and because" he "did not uphold" God's "holiness among the Israelites. Martin Luther King, Jr. did not enter the promise land, because evil infected the people in our nation, even the people of goodwill. We as a people are still waiting to occupy the land held by the giants. You may even say that we remain on the mountaintop looking at the Promised Land, because we have had some mountaintop experiences.

I say: Let us leave the mindset of the Promised Land and go to the reality of Calvary. The Lamb of God was crucified, but arose for the new life of believers. We are no longer in need of Canaan, we need the New Jerusalem.

Prayer: "Lord Jesus Christ, Son of God, grant mercy and healing upon us, who grieve. Amen."

Day 59

BRINGING THE BEST OUT OF THE WORST

Read: James 1

In December of 2009, a decision was made that transformed my deliverance of the Word in the local church. For the first time in thirty four years of preaching, I decided to preach from Genesis to Revelation within the same year. The sixty-six books of the Bible are meaningfully connected in purposes and proclamation of the promises of God.

From the Father of faith to the great, great grandmother of King David and ancestor of Jesus, the Christ (not named in the first eight books of the Bible, but acknowledged in Matthew 1:5) God is at work ushering in redemption by way of a wanderer and a prostitute. An awesome God is transforming the world by way of bringing the best out of the worst.

Enjoy reading the Word of God through each of the Books of the Bible as you join me in this journey of faith. Below find selected verses from Genesis to Ruth. Promise to stay with me through the Word, and I promise that God will deliver on the Word.

Now the Lord said to Abram. "Go from your country and your kindred and your father's house to the land that I will show you. I will make of you a great nation, and I will bless you, and make your name great, so that you will be a blessing. I will bless those who bless you, and the one who curses you I will curse; and in you all the families of the earth shall be blessed." (Genesis 12:1-3 NRSV)

The Lord passed before him, and proclaimed, "The Lord, a God merciful and gracious, slow to anger, and abounding in steadfast love and faithfulness, keeping steadfast love for the thousandth generation, forgiving iniquity and transgression and sin, yet by no means clearing the guilty, but visiting the iniquity of the parents upon the children's children, to the third and the fourth generation." And Moses quickly bowed his head toward the earth, and worshiped. He said, "If now I have found favor in your sight, O Lord, I pray, let the Lord go with us. Although this is a stiff-necked people, pardon our iniquity and our sin, and take us for your inheritance." (Exodus 34:8-9 NRSV)

Thus you shall keep my commandments and observe them: I am the Lord. You shall not profane my holy name, that I may be sanctified among the people of Israel: I am the Lord: I sanctify you, I who brought you out of the land of Egypt to be your God: I am the Lord. (Leviticus 22:31-33 NRSV)

And now, therefore, let the power of the Lord be great in the way that you promised when you spoke, saying: "The Lord is slow to anger, and abounding in steadfast love, forgiving iniquity and transgression, but by no means clearing the guilty, visiting the iniquity of the parents upon the children to the third and the fourth generation." Forgive the iniquity of this people according to the greatness of your steadfast love, just as you have pardoned this people, from Egypt even until now. (Numbers 14:17-19 NRSV)

When you go out to war against your enemies, and the Lord your God hands them over to you and take them captive, suppose you see among the captives a beautiful woman who you desire and want to marry, and so you bring her to your house: she shall shave her head, pare her nails, discard her captive's garb, and shall remain in your house a full month, mourning for her father and mother; after that you may go in to her and be her husband, and she shall be your wife. But if you are not satisfied with her, you shall let her go free and not sell her for money. You must not treat her as a slave, since you have dishonored her. (Deuteronomy 21:10-14 NRSV)

"...Be strong and courageous; for you shall put this people in possession of the land that I swore to their ancestors to give them. Only be strong and very courageous, being careful to act in accordance with all the law that my servant Moses commanded you; do not turn from it to the right hand or the left, so that you may be successful wherever you go. This book of the law shall not depart out of your mouth; you shall meditate on it day and night, so that you may be careful to act in accordance with all that is written in it. For then you shall make your way prosperous, and then you shall be successful. I hereby command you: Be strong and courageous; do not be frightened or dismayed, for the Lord your God is with you wherever you go." (Joshua 1:6-9 NRSV)

After Abimelech, Tola son of Puah, son of Dodo, a man of Issachar, who lived at Shamir in the hill country of Ephraim, rose to deliver Israel. He judged Israel twenty-three years. Then he died, and was buried at Shamir. After him came Jair the Gileaditee, who judged Israel twenty-two years. He had thirty sons who rode on thirty donkeys; and they had thirty towns, which are in the land of Gilead, and are called Havvothjair to this day. Jair died, and was buried in Kamon. (Judges 10:1-5 NRSV)

Then the woman said to Naomi, "Blessed be the Lord, who has not left you this day without next-of-kin; and may his name be renowned in Israel! He shall be to you a restorer of life and a nourished of your old age; for your daughter-in-law who loves you, who is more to you than seven sons, has borne him." Then Naomi took the child and laid him in her bosom, and became his nurse. The women of the neighborhood gave him a name, saying, "A son has been born to Naomi." They named him Obed; he became the father of Jesse, the father of David. (Ruth 4:14-17 NRSV)

Prayer: "Lord Jesus Christ, Son of God, grant mercy and healing upon us, who grieve. Amen."

Day 60

SUCCESS IN THE BATTLE OF LIFE

Read: First Peter 4

Mentored by Moses, Joshua feasted on the Book of Law as the Word of God, prospered and gained success in the battle of life. Leading the people of God into worship beyond the River of the place of their forefathers, Joshua challenged them to make up their minds to worship the gods of their forefathers or the gods of the Amorites or come unto the blessings worshipping God. One thing for sure, he knew that the key to success in the battle of life was to obey the commands of God, being "strong and very courageous". At some point in life a stand has to be taken, even when it is to be taken alone or with family. In his farewell address, Joshua announced that "... as for me and my house, we shall serve the Lord."

The battles of the Civil Rights Movement have been many. One civil rights leader has said: "We never won a battle we fail to fight, and we never lost a battle we fought." The current leaders in the Civil Rights Movement are agents of change facing old issues. Still on the table for discussion are among other things: housing foreclosures, student loans and credit card debts, the needs of the poor, political prisoners, heath care and heath disparities, etc. The battles are many, and the fight for social change often has few agents of change. People are often afraid to be change agents. Sometimes best of workers become tired or frustrated with the process or time requirements to change. Endurance and other attributes of power must abound in the courageous champions of social change.

Being successful as change agents in the social arena requires knowledge of the laws and facts surrounding life, strength to with stand those who oppose change to unjust laws, and courage to make change were change is possible. Change is still necessary in rural areas of the United States of America. Agricultural Secretary Tom Valsack announced the availability of $449 million to 128 businesses in rural areas of the nation. This represents the ability for persons with good ideas and valid skills to access the capital necessary to making positive change. People who have the right ideas, and recognize their weaknesses may hire persons more skilled as mentors to aid in their success with the capital being available. This is a project of hope for rural areas of the nation.

What about your concerns? No idea has to be a failure. The failure is in not trying to fulfill the dreams birthed from the idea. You have an idea? Gather all you need to know about the facts surrounding your idea. Then, negotiate and network with person able to help with the facilitation of your ideas. Sharpen your skills in the area of concern, and go for the bucks to make it happen. There are many ways to seek funding, so research until you settle on the best means for you. Above all of this, remember who to serve and worship.

The keys to success are not the monies or the popularity. The keys to success in the battles of life are: 1) Respect for God and the creativity given to you, 2) Striving to the fulfillment of the promise for your endeavor, 3) Recalling the teachings of your mentor, 4) Working the plan, so that the plan works for you, and 5) Be strong and courageous in taking the leap of faith. Victory may not be seen in the beginning. Holding on to the directives for success and working to bring about the changes necessary will lead into the fulfillment of the promise.

One of nicest young men known to me was murdered by two guys as he was driving home following a work day. His wife with two living children was five months in pregnancy with their third child. How you survive such destruction to the life of a love one and disruption to the family?

Thirty-six years prior to the murder of my nephew, I visioned surviving all things by faith. On the day of my brother's operation, I arose, knelt down on my knees and prayed a prayer I have never forgotten: "Lord God, don't let my brother die. Do not allow his face to be disfigured. He is so much better than I am. Let him live and take my life. Mother needs him. But, your will be done. So, if he is to die, grant me the strength to live for both of us. I promise to be good. And, if you allow both of us to live, I promise to preach for you all of my days. Please Lord, hear my promise" (following the Lord's Prayer, I said: "Amen"). I left school early that day and rushed back to the member's house. Later the call came that he was not only alive, but his face was not disfigured and they went in through the previous incision with no cancer found. I fought the battle of life with faith in God and won, right?

What about the chance to fight for my nephew? I learned in 2004 that fighting with the sword of the spirit is the greatest of weapons. When I work on Saturdays with a movement to free persons, who are unjustly imprisoned, I work with a transforming faith. When I walk the streets in the heat of the nights, I travel with a faith. This is the faith that yields success in the battle of life. It is a strong and courageous faith. A faith my nephew had to have in the midst of opposition to his life. I pray to God that my life will be a witness to his victory over death, because

I believe. Thus with my nephew's picture on this desk from where I type, I often say: "Nephew, like you, I am standing strong and courageous in faith. A faith your father helps me understand."

Prayer: "Lord Jesus Christ, Son of God, grant mercy and healing upon us, who grieve. Amen."

Day 61

BROTHERS

Read: Second Peter 1

Bishop Claude Rouse, Jr. and Bernard Jerome Rouse, Sr. are brothers. As of this writing, Bishop is a retired chemical engineer, who owns a finance business with Minnie Loney Rouse (his beloved wife) and Bernard is a retired bio-chemical engineer – called out of retirement by the company he worked with for several years. Both were born in Atlanta, Georgia a few years prior to my birth in Greenville, South Carolina. Though five to seven years their junior, I was taught from the same laptop of Mother, who gave birth to the sons of Bishop Claude Rouse, Sr. (January 20, 1920 – February 19, 2003). Bishop and Bernard continue to teach through the sincerity of heart, which our mother, Lula Alberta Woodbury Rouse (May 13, 1928 – April 15, 2002), taught would bond us to "stick like glue." My brothers teach love between brothers through it all.

In an email made public through Facebook, Bernard posted a note under the subject: "Stay Safe". Sensing the deep sincerity, I paused to prayerfully read his words of shame and pain with compassionate concern. Shame must we be to continue terrorism on our neighbors and relatives. Pain comes with the reality that "... there's trouble all around us these days ... one (you and I) must never take life for granted ..." Bernard noted that two men were taken from Huntsville, Alabama to medical facilities of the University of Alabama. While the University of Alabama football team heard fans cheer: "roll tide" as they became the National Football Champions in the NCAA, pause came upon us and we acknowledged two heroic sons as men of courage and honor, who were injured for the sake of our peace and safety. Because there are brothers and sisters enduring pain in battles, we are able to enjoy life, even athletic games.

I called our elder brother, Bishop, on that day to say: "I love you!" My brothers are my heroes. I was the son of the three to be given the responsibility of upholding God's purpose for preaching and teaching through our familial generation. Hiram Rouse was our great-grandfather, who witnessed the call of God upon his three sons out of twelve children (nine daughters) to preach. The fact that our father stood in the pulpit as did his father – Hiram Bishop and his uncles Julius and Pilgrim reveals the anticipated call on the lives of the Rouse men and God has called each of us. Bishop, Jr. taught us in the 1960s that we may take diverse paths in faith-sharing. We will not each be in the pulpit, but we shall be through Jesus Christ faith-sharers. One morning, on a road to Lancaster, SC traveling to work from his home, which was in Shelby, NC, Bishop, Jr. wrecked into a tree and almost lost his life. When rescued, he asked: "Did I miss hitting the dog?" Our mother (diaconal minister in the United Methodist Church) had taught us to share in the responsibility of caring for living creatures (Genesis 1:24) and the love within the heart of my brother would not permit the killing of a dog in need of rescue. During his weeks in the hospital, Bernard was at Bishop's side to assure proper care as our brother recovered following the rescue.

I am the brother ordained by the United Methodist Church for ministry of Word, Sacrament and Service. However, the heroic preachers and teachers in my life are my BROTHERS, the practical ministers, who too, were taught by the catalyst of the Laptop Theologian to be teachers in peacemaking.

Prayer: "Lord Jesus Christ, Son of God, grant mercy and healing upon us, who grieve. Amen."

Day 62

FELLOWSHIP & COMPANIONSHIP

Read: First John 1

Mary lived as a most cherished sister-in-law to Marie. Through the years from Mary's age of 15 until her death in December of 2013 Mary and Marie were sincere friends. Michael Jackson sung a song: "Gone, too Soon", which rings true for those beloved in times of lives ended. Age aside, it is love that matters to the heart not the years of it…pure love is timeless. The lost of a beloved is ageless, too, as feelings carry on endlessly. Marie sobbed, when her mother called with the news that Mary, Marie's fellowship friend of a sister nature had died. Intense crying from the deepest part of Marie with streams of tears and screams from pain flooded our home. It was as though life ended the moment she heard the sad, very sad news: "Marie, Mary just died." No rationale could bring calm; no therapeutic theories would provide relief; no pastoral theology of care was to be applied…a spouse caring enough to listen and respect the need to cry…came to mind.

To Marie, Mary was more than sister-in-law or mere friend; she was a real representation of the forgiveness and fellowship Christ desires for the human experience of life. Marie spoke through her tears the hurt felt in desiring to speak again to the one person she turned to for conversation in times of uncertainty and difficulty. What then has to happen, in order to ease the agony of death?

Time continued and to continue in time, my wife freely shed tears until crying was not enough. Beyond the tears, the need to talk came. Avenues for conversation were made possible by every technological means necessary. Cell phone; land phone; laptop; desk top; etc…along with face to face and congregational doors were open for Marie to share her memories, her thoughts and whatever came to her that helped unload the grief. Who was I?

I was the life among the living. The life support there in the time of experiencing the unexpected and undesirable. And I write this in this book, so that others may be life among the living, when the experiences of death come close enough to be felt in the heart of the one with whom you share life and love. It is easy to just be life, when living life in Christ, who is the source of eternal life. I found that being present was life supportive and a source of revealing the life giving company of Jesus Christ. I did not have to be a sermon or husband or friend or consoler; I only needed to live and be life in the midst of the storm, when life seemed to have gone in the wind with the lost of such a friend as Mary.

Mary was gone, too soon to Mary and everyone desirous of her presence even now. I am one among the living, who continues life. Even the life of Mary is continued with the life of me, because I, too, love the life of Mary unto eternity. When death comes and you live on, be life for those around you...just be life not words or answers or anything more than life giving in times of the departure of human being. Be a life that ushers in companionship and fellowship in the midst of grief.

Prayer: "Lord Jesus Christ, Son of God, grant mercy and healing upon us, who grieve. Amen."

Day 63

TRUTH

Read: Second John 1-4

He may be remembered as a captain for life or a member of the Hall of Fame or a champion in the cause against concussions. He captained his team to be the best in the world. He inspired those privileged to be among his friends in college to believe in themselves as more than winners, because they are champions. Among the best to ever play the game, still the game is not why he is in my hall of friends.

Compassion filled his eyes as he spoke that his brother, who was a preacher had died. It was a respect for life that was inspiring. He had driven from his home over one hour from the church to share in support care for youth. He is a man of true heart. Therefore, I knew true to his word he would come speak to youth, whenever asked and time permitted. What I learned on his third of six annual visits was the respect, care and deep love he felt for his brother. He spoke profoundly to our youth that day about more than the game, The "Captain for Life" shared the importance of life and family.

I have heard no better discourse on the responsible care of physical life and being available in relationships with people – family. I thought: "My friend could be anywhere in the world. He would be paid thousands of dollars for giving five minutes of time to speak on the subjects in his life. Yet, he has come here as a friend, who is making himself available because we are responsible for lives of youth and children, who follow our steps."

Truth is we, you and I, are among the family of God. Created in the image of the Divine, we have the responsibility to compassion one another. "The captain" spoke in physical voice and in grief. The human loss of his brother delivered a new message. The message of Truth: Each moment that you live breathe love in and love out as a genuine self.

When accepting the reality of death among us, give genuine of yourself to persons, who will sincerely receive the authentic you.

Prayer: "Lord Jesus Christ, Son of God, grant mercy and healing upon us, who grieve. Amen."

Day 64

LOVE, WALK, HELP & WITNESS

Read: Third John

He is without a doubt the closest male friend of my lifetime. Born one month and four days in the same year, but after my birth, one could say we were born brothers of different mothers. In fact, we attributed to our friendship the labels of "foster brothers". Our parents and families acknowledged us in the same vein. I love him and call him my beloved friend.

This is a tribute to our walk as brothers attempting to make a true difference in the world. We traveled across seas together…danced in Europe and Africa with people he introduced to me having been a world traveler for some time. What's essential is that no friend on earth shared the compassion for helping others more mutually in ministries, including the ministry of death and dying.

We helped each other through many of the deepest experiences of pain – deaths of our parents. I felt the air deflating life from him and observed his process of recovery. His strength in the midst of the reality of death and dying rose with each blow of the wind. Why?

His family is built on a solid foundation as people of God. They live the faith taught and preached through their heritage of hope. It is not just remarkable, it is miraculous. Speaking of the miraculous, times came when his life experience would be to defeat threat of physical cessation not once but twice. With a supportive wife there was never a moment of giving up on the life. Prayer was never too much and love was never more enormous than the love ushered unto him by a wife, who is his closest friend and a model spouse.

Life support is important in marital love, daily walk, help and witness of the two becoming one. Leaning with a unity of faith, hope and love that glorifies God through life is how a spouse may provide life support.

The last dance that we attend with our friends will not be on earth. Shall we never dance in the company of one another in this life; may we witness one another dance with the Lord of the dance in eternity.

Prayer: "Lord Jesus Christ, Son of God, grant mercy and healing upon us, who grieve. Amen."

Day 65

THE FALLEN

Read: Jude

Grief recovery is necessitated by reality of the fallen.

Person murdered, during Bible Study shook the nation, a total shock to the majority of people in the world. There was no warning sign. In the aftermath, there remained the struggle to believe it happen.

It is being archived a massacre. When reports came across news channels, I thought: "There needs to be a transformation in socialization. A positive change in the relatedness of persons to persons is the only way to stop hate crimes." Yes, I gave thought to striving to end hate, so with genuine intentionality I discerned it best that I practiced self-control against the enemy of peace. Thoughts grew to desire forgiveness and reconciliation verses punishment of guilt. The decision was to do the necessary to denounce violence and promote world peace by partnering with leaders in opposition to hate crimes.

Have you experience of loss. Loss by any means may lead to a deepening in grief. Take action against the grief not people accused of causing the grief. How?

Start with a small or large group setting for discussion purposes. Formulate your questions and be open to responding to the question of others. It is human to have questions in the midst of grief. The plan is to talk through the tears, so that in time the touches upon the heart and mind may become safely therapeutic and healing.

Through over forty years of pastoral ministry, the experiences controlled questioning in recovery group has been effective in assisting persons in formulating a map to recovery. Local churches can successfully and effectively build grief recovery teams and host grief recovery gatherings. Below are six grief recovery questions that can be used effectively in large or small grief recovery groups or in private self-care.

1. How does the experience of loss present a challenge to the future?

2. On a scale of 1 to 10 with 10 being the highest state of readiness to meet the challenges; rate the state of readiness for changes throughout your life in respect to your loss. Discuss why the rating is lower even though the rating may be one.

3. After discussing state of readiness, what or who do you believe presents obstacles to readiness for the changes? Is it possible to address those obstacles and/or move those people? How?

4. What are the commitments necessary to grief recovery on the given loss in realities of your household?

5. Looking at the state of readiness for change, what would change look like when action to move forward is taken? What is the next step?

6. How would a time of healing and guidance on grief recovery eliminate quilt and shame as the pain and confusion continues?

The heart may need time before singing again. A new song may not come at once. Thus, patience in time is a good practice. No matter how you seek to fix it, give it attention and in time it can become a sustainable healing of fallen hearts.

Prayer: "Lord Jesus Christ, Son of God, grant mercy and healing upon us, who grieve. Amen."

Day 66

WHO, THE ALMIGHTY

Read: Revelation

God! Always with God is the way to recovery from experiences of living. All things, good and bad in life, no matter what it is has chance to recover from what harms and hurts, if we share openly with God. Life is given and supplied by God. The source of life support through every circumstance need not be searched out, because our mere existence is grounded and secured in the reality of being. We are, because God is. In my experiences of living, I share all with God. Yes, God...

This one is for you. In adoration and awe, I thank you for the gift of love, joy and peace. I want the world to know the essential reason to rise in mornings and rest during nights. It is as though the rule of life has the practical line up for intensifying delight with existence. Never wanting life to stop...here and now I affirm the gift of eternal life.

Praying through the days with sincerity of heart, I shall work in appreciation from beginning to the end of life with you. I am leaping in faith. Yes, I believe in you and want you to know my soul feels inspired as my mind holds focus on what was given to me from birth – life. This is an eternal blessing. In witness to the world, I close this witness in affirmation of faith.

I believe in God, the Father almighty,
creator of heaven and earth.
I believe in Jesus Christ, his only Son, our Lord,
who was conceived by the Holy Spirit,
born of the Virgin Mary,
suffered under Pontius Pilate,
was crucified, died, and was buried;
he descended to the dead.
On the third day he rose again;
he ascended into heaven,
he is seated at the right hand of the Father,
and he will come to judge the living and the dead.
I believe in the Holy Spirit,
the holy catholic Church,
the communion of saints,
the forgiveness of sins,
the resurrection of the body,
and the life everlasting.
Amen. (The Apostles' Creed)

I am not a lone participant in conversations with God. Marie and I often talk about conversing with God. It is an experience of ease to be able to share faith with my wife. Sharing life in the midst of grief is a reality. She ask many questions never posed before. A question that is for the records and annals of our experience of God is: "Will you promise me to live forever?" It is not strange or insane to search for peace before and after life storms. At times the place of peace is a get away from the experience of hurt felt from human loss. The human heart and mind seeks blessed assurance away from disruptions to peace. We desire the experience of love to be everlasting. My answer to her question was, is and shall be: "Yes, I promise you to live forever away from the valley of tears and into the hands of God. Come with me." Grief recovery is divine, when two-fold: shared with God and human souls. Don't be alone throughout life...share life with God and be blessed in sharing with the godly gift of love ones.

Prayer: "Lord Jesus Christ, Son of God, grant mercy and healing upon us, who grieve. Amen."

Conclusion

In conclusion, grief recovery as a ministry has validity in the Christian tradition. In fact, every faith group may develop ways and means of caring for persons, who are lachrymose due to the existential loss in the human experience of life and death. In addition to the thoughts and feelings, which this book aimed to guide, funeral; memorial; and remembrance services intend to celebrate lives and heal the mourners. The messages of Scripture and support of people can assist in the process of grief recovery as well as heal the disconsolate. Below is an outline for the gathering of a supportive sacred community, which may be used too with sincerity of heart in annual observances or as often as desired for comfort to those who mourn.

WELCOME: (A host shall greet persons attending with sincere gratitude for the presence of each participant. The welcome should be brief, yet personable and warm.)

Holy Communion: (Recommended) It is good to share communion before going into grief processing, so as to claim victory over the death.

Meditation: - "Destination of The Living" Job 30:23 (10 minutes) Delivered by a person of faith.

In the midst of teaching, I felt as though breath was leaving my body. It was nearing 3:00 PM on a Thursday. Later the same night, I would learn that during the afternoon, my close friend took his last breath in life and his spirit flew into eternity. The reaction of my heart was yearning for a "day of prayer."

Days come and go. Each day provides opportunity for communication with God. What makes a day of prayer different from other days in life? The difference is in the intent of the praying. During "a day of prayer", an individual is intentional about having solitude seeking the will of God beyond the experience of grief. Lord, what shall I do?

The difference in praying everyday and a day of prayer is in the quantity even more than the quality. It is a day of conscious and constant praying throughout the day for every activity and action.

You are invited during your day of praying without ceasing to commune with the Spirit of God. Communication throughout designated time sensing the Divine Presence from beginning to end pray as an individual in recovery.

1. Praying in thanksgiving for another day among living human beings having possibilities and opportunities for lives shared with relatives, friends, associates, neighbors, etc.
2. Praying for the faith community.
3. Praying for the business community.
4. Praying for the past, present and future.
5. Praying for sitting and traveling; standing and walking.
6. Praying for every second of the day.
7. Praying for clergy; chaplains, pastors, counselors, young and old in training or ordained. Praying...
8. Praying grace over food; blessings over meetings; covering of protection in departures. Praying...
9. Praying peace in relations; fresh winds of the Spirit in new communications. Praying...
10. Praying for the schools, children, parents, administrators, personnel, volunteers, etc...

In 1995, Ray Sherman Anderson wrote a book on Self Care: A Theology of Personal Empowerment and Spiritual Healing. The focus on self is important for pastoral care and counseling. Knowing about the self and how God empowers human beings into a divine image is a key in effective shepherding. Self-care has to do with experiencing self-worth, building emotional health, and embracing a vital faith. Henri Nouwen became known for his many works on solitude. One of them geared especially toward priest is his work on The Wounded Healer. These men point out from protestant and catholic perspectives the reality of human hurt experienced in the lives of servants and shepherds. The works give insight into how healers serve through the pain of personal wounds.

Out of experiences of lost, hurt, and abuse may come shepherds attending to the people of God. They serve humbly without arrogance or sense of superiority.

With sincerity of heart they give from unique self-experience of reality. In the discovery of authentic self-experiences of wounds and the healing of wounds; pastors and lay servants may be empowered to work beyond brokenness. As "wounded healers", they come to know the reality of healing, guiding, sustaining, reconciling and nurturing as defined by Howard Clinebell in the Basic Types of Pastoral Care and Counseling.

Praying: O Lord God, receive our words of request and provide mercy, grace and love, so that our day of prayer will end in a night of prayer fulfilled. Amen.

Next: <u>A Theological Perspective on Grief Recovery</u> by the pastor or "The Laptop Theologian."

Luonne Abram Rouse